Rafael Nadal: The Inspiring Story of One of Tennis' Greatest Legends

An Unauthorized Biography

D1664701

By: Clayton Geoffreys

Visit my website at www.claytongeoffreys.com

Cover photo by Tatiana Kulitat is licensed under CC BY 2.0 / modified from original

Table of Contents

Foreword

In the Open Era of tennis, we have been fortunate to see some of the greatest to ever play the game. Since 2000, men's tennis has been largely dominated by three individuals: Roger Federer, Novak Djokovic, and Rafael Nadal. In this book, we'll detail the story of Rafael Nadal and his journey of greatness. Often nicknamed "The King of Clay", Nadal is one of, if not the most dominant clay-court player to grace the court. Thank you for purchasing *Rafael Nadal: The Inspiring Story of One of Tennis' Greatest Legends*. In this unauthorized biography, we will learn Rafael Nadal's incredible life story and impact on the game of tennis. Hope you enjoy and if you do, leave a review!

Also, check out my website at claytongeoffreys.com to join my exclusive list where I let you know about my latest books. To thank you for your purchase, you can go to my site to download a free copy of *33 Life Lessons: Success Principles, Career Advice & Habits of Successful People*. In the book, you'll learn from some of the greatest thought leaders of different industries on what it takes to become successful and how to live a great life.

Cheers,

Clayton Geoffreys

Introduction

In the early part of the 21st century, Spain has provided the world with two significant contributions to the sports world. One lasted for nearly a decade, and the second continues to amaze as he enters the twilight of his career.

The first is the Spanish national soccer team, who revolutionized the way the game is played thanks to their "tiki-taka" style of quick passing in triangles, emphasis on possession, and intelligent runs into space that stretched opposing defenses. A group of stars led by Andres Iniesta, Xavi, Gerard Pique, Sergio Ramos and many others had an unprecedented amount of success as they bracketed a 2010 World Cup title with European Championship crowns in both 2008 and 2012.

The aesthetic beauty of the tiki-taka in which players feint and move in rapid succession as the ball is effortlessly caressed around the pitch is a stark contrast to the violent beauty of Spain's other notable sports export, tennis star Rafael Nadal.

A naturally talented yet self-made player, Nadal has turned one of the hardest-hit two-handed shots in the game into a cottage industry of success. His 15 Grand Slam titles are second all-time to arguably the greatest player in the sport's history and his generational peer Roger Federer. His unrivaled dominance of the clay-court surface, highlighted by his record 10 French Open titles, did not just harken the names of Bjorn Borg and Mats Wilander to tennis historians. They also fall in line without debate behind the man known as "Rafa," a spitfire of energy who punctuates his key points with a fist pump and a cry of "Vamos!"

In a period when men's tennis was blessed with three of its greatest players, here is the story of the man who not only challenged greatness but became great himself in the process. This is the story of Rafael Nadal Parera.

Chapter 1: Early Life and Childhood

Rafael Nadal Parera was born June 3, 1986, in Manacor, Spain. He is the oldest of two children to parents Sebastian and Ana Maria Parera, with a younger sister, Maria Isabel.[1] Manacor is the second-largest city on the Spanish island of Mallorca, and the first municipality on the island is estimated to have been established around the year 1200.[2] It is part of the Balearic Islands and located in the Mediterranean Sea to the east of mainland Spain almost directly south of Barcelona.[3]

There is sporting lineage in Nadal's family. One of his uncles, Miguel Angel Nadal, was a tough soccer player who played for both club and country. He worked his way up from the local club team CD Manacor to the biggest club on the island, Real Mallorca, a team that played at the top level of Spanish football, La Liga.[4] Though the team sometimes struggled to stay in the top flight, Nadal stood out as a bruising defender who had the skills to distribute the ball from his center back position. Nadal's versatility allowed him to play in the midfield, and those skills caught the attention of Spain's most prestigious club, Barcelona, as well as the national team, nicknamed "La Furia Roja."[5]

Nadal would eventually join the Catalan team in 1991, and that season, Barcelona won both the domestic title in Spain and the European club championship. He became a key player the following season as Barca again enjoyed local success, but the team was overrun by Italian side AC Milan 4-0 in the 1994 European Cup final.[6]

Later that summer, he represented Spain in the 1994 World Cup in the United States, but his time in the tournament ended almost as quickly as it began. "The Beast of Barcelona" was ejected in the 25th minute of his team's first game in group play against South Korea for a hard tackle that denied a clear scoring opportunity.[7] The match ended in a 2-2 draw, but the red card meant that Nadal was suspended for the next game. He would eventually return for the knockout rounds, but Spain was eliminated by Italy on a late goal by Roberto Baggio in the quarterfinals.[8]

With one uncle enjoying a high-profile sporting career, young Rafael had a second uncle, Toni. A multi-sport star, Toni Nadal took a liking to tennis after watching Ilie Năstase play. He quickly rose to prominence as a teenager and was among the top 30 players in the country, but his father asked him to stop playing and concentrate on academics. Toni Nadal acquiesced to his father's wishes but also got his tennis coaching license so he could teach the sport.[9]

The Nadal household was across the street from the tennis club in Manacor, and young Rafael would join the group of kids at the age of 3. Toni Nadal quickly realized the potential of his nephew, who showed the ability to hit balls both left and right-handed.[10] He also used a two-handed swing, something which was not unique at the time, but it was something Toni also realized would at some point limit his nephew's potential.

Like all loving uncles, Toni picked on Rafael to make a point to the other kids, making him clean up at the end of sessions. Uncle also told nephew that he should swing his forehand with his left hand since he felt that was Rafael's dominant hand.[11] In an ironic twist, it would turn out hitting a tennis ball would be about the only important thing Rafael Nadal would do left-handed.

Toni Nadal realized Rafael had the potential to be a professional tennis player and convinced his nephew's parents to begin pursuing this path. Young Rafa was practicing five times a week for 90 minutes at a time, and that work ethic instilled at a young age paid immediate dividends as eight-year-old Rafael Nadal won the 12-and-under regional title on the Balearic Islands.[12]

At the age of 10, Toni began to transition his nephew from hitting his forehand with two hands to hitting it with one. All the while, Rafael was also a burgeoning soccer player, showing an ability to score goals at the forward position. He might not be the second "Beast of Barcelona" like Uncle Miguel on the back line, but there was enough talent that Rafael could be a two-sport star.[13] At age 11, though, Rafael was asked to choose between tennis and soccer since his new soccer coach would not let the youngster miss matches to participate in tennis tournaments. Given that Nadal had already established himself as one of the best young players in the country, winning the under-12 age group and finishing runner-up in the under-14 age group, selecting tennis was an easy decision.

"He had a very good mentality," Toni Nadal recalled. "So I thought it was possible, not probable, but possible that he could win a Grand Slam."[14]

With his commitment to tennis meant an expanded coaching circle as Toni Nadal was joined by Toni Colom in Palma, which was Manacor's largest city.[15] The two plotted how to make young Rafael a better player. He was good at many aspects of the game but had no one standout feature. Given that he was physically mature, Toni Nadal worked to give his nephew a solid base of fundamentals, but they would take the time to make Rafa's forehand his go-to shot.

"First hit the ball hard; then we'll see about keeping the ball in," his uncle said.[16]

Toni Nadal's other important job besides coach was to keep young Rafa grounded. He mixed praise with reality, reminding his nephew of just how tough it was to be not only a good tennis player but also a successful one. He also instilled Rafa's work ethic with the simple ethos of "however long it takes to do something is how long it takes to get done."

"If you have to train two hours, you train two hours; if you have to train five, you train five; if you have to repeat an exercise fifty thousand times, you do it," he said. "That's what separates the champions from the merely talented... the greater the effort, the greater the value."[17]

At age 14, the Nadal family reached another crossroads. The Spanish Tennis Federation felt that it was time for Rafael to take the next step and train in Barcelona. For the Nadal family, this was a frightening prospect because it would break up their tight-knit family. Rafael's father was concerned about his son's education while Uncle Toni was concerned his nephew's playing skills would regress.[18]

The family opted against sending Rafael to the big city, and with good reason. In addition to the practice time with Toni in Manacor, the young Nadal was also getting practice time with Carlos Moya, the 1998 French Open champion who also was ranked number 1 in the world at one point during his career.

"I could see by the sheer intensity with which he trained that he was super-ambitious and desperate to improve," Moya recounted. "What was certain about Rafa was that he was something different."[19]

So instead of the bright lights of Barcelona, it was the entire Nadal family, including Rafael's grandparents, in a block of apartments in Manacor. As Toni would later say, "The advantage of staying with his family was big for Rafael. It was a plus both in terms of tranquility and organization."[20]

Chapter 2: Teenage Years and Early Pro Career

At the tender age of 14, Nadal quietly began his professional tennis career, entering Futures events throughout Spain. But he found only limited success in these games and failed to reach the main draw of any of the ten tournaments he entered in a nine-month span of 2001.[1] It was not until he received a wild card to enter the main draw of an ITF Futures event in Seville that Nadal posted his first victory that mattered.

He defeated Spaniard Israel Matos Gil, ranked 751st in the world, by a 6-4, 6-4 scoreline in a clay-court tournament. It gave him five ATP Tour points, which was enough to enter him in the rankings for the first time at number 1,002.[2] Nadal would lose the next match respectably, a three-setter to Italy's Stefano Galvani, who was ranked 161st in the world.[3]

By April the following year, Nadal had climbed to 762nd in the world and entered the Mallorca Open as a wild card. Here he recorded his first ATP Tour victory impressively, upsetting world number 81 Ramon Delgado 6-4, 6-4. Still shy of his 16th birthday, Nadal would lose to Oliver Rochus in the next round, but he still had his first payday of nearly $6,000.[4]

Later that year, Nadal would accept another wild card, this time to compete in the Junior Wimbledon. His first appearance at the all-

England club would be one to remember as he started out by upsetting number 2 seed Brian Dabul of Argentina in three sets.[5] Straight-set victories followed in the next two rounds before another upset, this time of number 8 Philipp Petzschner of Germany in the quarterfinals.[6] While his run would end in the semis versus Lamine Ouahab of Algeria, playing well in a future tournament that included fellow future pros Jo-Wilfried Tsonga, Marcos Baghdatis, and Tomas Berdych did wonders for Nadal's confidence.[7]

After Wimbledon, he won six Futures titles, including the last two of the season to crack the Top 200 in the tour rankings.[8] That success carried over into 2003 when he made the finals of three separate Challenger events. That was enough to get him into the main draw in Monte Carlo, where he posted victories over Karol Kucera and Alberto Costa, who was ranked seventh in the world and also the reigning French Open champion.[9]

Now comfortably inside the Top 100 on the ATP Tour, Nadal made his first appearance in the main draw of a Grand Slam event as he entered Wimbledon. The Spaniard acquitted himself well, defeating Mario Ancic and Lee Childs before a straight-set loss to 12th-seeded Paradorn Srichaphan as he became the youngest player to reach the third round at SW19 since Boris Becker in 1984.[10]

Nadal would shuttle back and forth between Challenger events and the ATP Tour, losing to Moya in the semifinals in Croatia and reaching the second round of the U.S. Open. He finished the year with a 14-11 record on the ATP Tour, but won almost $250,000 despite barely cracking .500.[11]

2004 would mark Nadal's first full-time season on the ATP Tour. He came close to his first title in Auckland, losing to Dominik Hrbaty in the final.[12] While Nadal was making his first Australian Open appearance, Federer was en route to winning the title and claiming the world's number 1 spot for the first time in his career. Meanwhile, the Spaniard had another respectable showing and reached the third round before running into hometown favorite Lleyton Hewitt.[13]

The Aussie needed a pair of tiebreakers to beat back a challenge from the Spanish teen before finishing him off 6-2 in the third set. Still, the fight Nadal put up caught the attention of Hewitt, a two-time Grand Slam champion and former world number 1.

"He's a hell of a player," Hewitt said. "It was a lot tougher than I expected. I really had to raise my game."[14]

Nadal then made his Davis Cup debut, splitting his singles matches versus Jiri Novak (loss) and Radek Stepanek (win). He met Federer for the first time in the third round of the Masters Series in Miami, stunning the world number 1 with a thorough 6-3, 6-3 victory on the hardcourt.[15] Now a Top 40 player who had acquired the nickname "The Prodigy," Federer gave the teen sensation his dues.

"He hit some really incredible shots, and that's what youngsters do," the Swiss star said. "I've heard a lot about him and saw some of his matches, so this is not a big surprise."[16]

He finally broke through for his first ATP Tour title in Sopot, Poland. Nadal was seeded sixth in a relatively strong field that included Marat Safin and Nikolay Davydenko as the top two seeds. But Nadal's path was cleared with the help of some upsets. All of the seeded players in his half of the draw, Safin, number 4 Igor Andreev, and number 7 Albert Montanes were all eliminated in the first round.

Still, Nadal rolled through his opponents in straight sets all the way to the final where he faced Argentine Jose Acasuso. The Spaniard was at his best on the defensive, turning away 11 of Acasuso's 12 break point opportunities. In turn, Nadal was able to convert three of his own, and the 6-3, 6-4 victory made the 18-year-old Nadal the youngest player to win the ATP Tour title since Hewitt won his maiden crown in Adelaide in 1998.[17]

No longer able to hide behind potential as a tour winner, Nadal returned to New York for his second U.S. Open appearance. He was no match for defending champion and number 2 seed Andy Roddick, who tore through him for a 6-0, 6-3, 6-4 win. The match took only 97 minutes, and while the scoreline was lopsided, Roddick knew more than enough that he would have another final in the future.

"I think he's a lot more confident than he's letting on if he said he didn't have a clue," Roddick said when asked about the platitudes

Nadal offered after the match. "He's got more of a clue than any 18-year-old I've ever seen."[18]

That clue became readily apparent when the two met again in the Davis Cup final in Spain, where Nadal posted a four-set victory on the red clay of Seville in the second singles match to help power his country to the title.

"I think he can be a great champion," said Moya, who served as his teammate for the international tie. "He's the kind of guy that likes to play these kinds of matches. So I really trust him. I believe in him."[19]

After his first breakthrough at the international level, Grand Slam success still eluded him early in 2005. He got a round further in Melbourne, but the same opponent sent him packing again. Hewitt needed all five sets this time after winning the first two, battling through a hip injury in a four-hour match as part of his stunning run to the final. Still, after a second straight year of fending off the Spanish teen, Hewitt was well aware Nadal's time was coming. And fast.

"Nadal's got a great attitude for tennis," he said, adding, "he is hungry and good for the game. He's gonna be around for a while."[20]

Few would realize just how prescient those words would turn out to be.

Chapter 3: Nadal's First Grand Slam Title, the 2005 French Open

There was no shame in losing to the hometown favorite Hewitt in five sets in his backyard in Melbourne. It was his deepest run in a Grand Slam tournament, and he had moved inside the Top 50 in the ATP Tour rankings.[1] He moved on to South America, reaching the quarterfinals in Buenos Aires before winning his first title of the year in Sao Paulo, defeating compatriot Alberto Martin in three sets in the final.[2] After another title in Mexico, he was now ranked 31st.

The scene shifted to the hardcourt Masters Series in the U.S. where he squandered a two-set lead to Federer in the finals in Miami.[3] Nadal gained confidence ahead of the French Open with titles in Monte Carlo and Barcelona, which were the first of many such trophies to fill the cupboards. A five-set win over Guillermo Coria to win the Rome Masters extended his clay-court winning streak to 17 matches.[4] The five-set victory, which also foreshadowed Nadal's endurance, clocked in at 5 hours and 14 minutes. He suddenly found himself in the top five in the ATP Tour rankings and nipping at Federer's heels.

"I have won three consecutive titles. I don't know how to explain that. I am playing well, and I have a lot of confidence, obviously," the Spanish teenager said. "I just want to continue at this level. Every time I win a match, they ask me if I am the favorite for Roland Garros, but the favorite for Ronald Garros will be the player who plays the best there."[5]

Nadal entered the primary field in Paris for the first time as the fourth seed behind Federer, Andy Roddick, and Marat Safin. It would also turn out to be the final French Open appearance for sixth-seeded American Andre Agassi. Nadal's section of the draw contained two seeded French players, Richard Gasquet and Sebastien Grosjean as well as number 16 seed Radek Stepanek of the Czech Republic.

His first opponent was Germany's Lars Burgsmüller on Court 1, which many likened to a bullring because of its round features. In some ways that was fitting because the media likened Nadal to a "matador" because of his unique look and fashion sense.[6] Burgsmüller was ranked 97th in the world but put up little resistance in a straight-set loss. It would be the first of many such victories Nadal recorded at Roland Garros, but it would be remembered as the only time he did not play on the two highest-profile courts there.[7]

Next up was Belgian Xavier Malisse. Despite a spotty first serve that he placed in just 51 percent of the time, Nadal compensated by jumping all over Malisse's second serve and wound up breaking the Belgian seven times in a straight-set victory.[8] The third round Nadal would have to deal with a partisan crowd for the first time as he faced Gasquet, the 30th seed.

The two teenagers had met in the semifinals at Monte Carlo where Nadal rallied to win in three sets. There would be no such drama this time as the Frenchman won just nine games total before being vanquished.[9] On the bottom half of Nadal's sectional draw, Grosjean had eliminated Stepanek to set up a fourth-round showdown that would give the winner passage into the final eight.

The match took two days to complete because of rain, and Nadal caused a stir by criticizing the fans for their lack of etiquette. He had questioned a call, and the fans at Chatrier Court responded with jeers and whistles that took nearly five minutes to subside.[10] He also felt that Grosjean was winding up the crowd, which had been in a frenzied mood since they voted against a European constitution.[11]

The draw then opened some for Nadal when compatriot David Ferrer stunningly defeated reigning French Open champion Gaudio by rallying from 0-4 down in the fifth set.[12] But the stirring win left Ferrer empty for his match against the Spanish teen as Nadal made quick work of him in straight sets.[13]

Nadal advanced to face top-seeded Federer in the semifinals, heady stuff for a player just celebrating his 19th birthday. The Swiss star was seeking to complete a career Grand Slam, a quest that everyone now knows took much longer than it should have because of Nadal's dominance in Paris. But at this very moment, he was just a precocious teen trying to take down the world's number 1 player and blow out his candles afterwards.

Nadal set the tone of the match, breaking Federer in the first game. It would be the first of four breaks the Mallorcan would convert as he took the first set 6-3. Still, Federer was unruffled. He had come back to defeat Nadal in more dire circumstances in Florida that spring, rallying from 1-4 in the fifth set to complete a stirring comeback.[14]

And that savvy showed in the second set as he sprang to life, aided by a brief rain delay. The youthfulness of Nadal was also on full display, breaking Federer almost out of spite to extend the second set to make it 5-2.[15] That spark grew as Nadal continued to pin Federer to his backhand, slowing the game down and he grabbed a break to go up 4-2. Federer would break right back the following game, but Nadal seized the momentum of the match with a powerful running forehand on his third break point that also clinched the third set.[16]

As the sun began to retreat, time was of the essence. The two players held serve for seven games in the fourth set before Federer's backhand failed him as Nadal grabbed a 5-3 lead. Then it was the forehand that deserted him on match point, and the Spaniard would enjoy his just desserts with his most famous victory to that point in his burgeoning career.[17]

"It's incredible to be in the final and beat the number one in the world," said Nadal, who became the youngest French Open finalist since Michael Change got there at age 17 in 1989. "Being in the final is a dream. I've just beaten the man who is number one to me, not only for his tennis, but also as a person."[18]

After the highest of highs in beating Federer, Nadal would face a virtual unknown in Argentine Mariano Puerta in the final. Puerta was unseeded entering the tournament, but he began his startling run with an upset of 13th-seeded Ivan Ljubičić in the first round. Along the way, he also ended Stan Wawrinka's maiden French Open appearance in four sets in the third round, and then beat number 9 Guillermo Cañas and number 12 Nikolay Davydenko in five sets in the quarters and semis to be Nadal's unlikely opponent.

It was the first time two left-handers were in the French Open final since 1946, and Puerta showed few nerves in his first Grand Slam final, rallying to win the opening set via tiebreaker.[19] Nadal asserted his expected dominance in the second set, breaking the Argentine for a 3-1 lead in the second set and three more times in the third set to grab control of the match.

Still, Puerta did not go down quickly. He earned three set points in a bid to extend the match to a decisive fifth set, but Nadal scrambled from a 15-40 deficit to square the set at 5-all.[20] Now fully spent, Nadal was able to close out the match without a tiebreak as Puerta launched a forehand wide on match point.

The jubilant Nadal had energy to spare after expending it for nearly 3 ½ hours, shaking hands with the King of Spain and bouncing about like the teenager he was after a historic victory. He became the first player to win the French Open in his first appearance since Mats Wilander in 1982 and set an Open Era record for teenagers by extending his winning streak to 24 matches.[21]

"I played with my best head and my best tennis," Nadal said. "He (Puerta) played unbelievably, and there were times I thought I might lose."[22]

In retrospect, that quote looks so comically naïve given the reign of dominance it ushered in for Nadal at Roland Garros. While many people expected the young Spaniard to add to his Grand Slam haul, few imagined it would wind up being such a haul.

Chapter 4: Nadal's Rise to Stardom

After his Grand Slam breakthrough, it took a while for Nadal to overcome that championship hangover. He lost his first match post-Roland Garros, a three-setter, to unheralded and 147th-ranked Alexander Waske in a Wimbledon tune-up in Germany. Nadal fared little better at the all-England club despite being the number 4 seed, losing to Luxembourg's Gilles Muller in the second round.[1]

He quickly put aside the disappointment of Wimbledon in Switzerland, winning on the clay of Båstad by dropping one set in five matches. Nadal quickly followed with another championship, this time in Stuttgart in a similar fashion. He extended his winning streak to 16 matches with a third successive title, capturing the Canada Masters by defeating Andre Agassi in three sets in the final.[2]

That win streak would end the following week with an upset loss to Tomas Berdych in Cincinnati, but he appeared primed for the U.S. Open. Nadal entered New York as the second seed to Federer, and he made quick work of American wild-cards Bobby Reynolds and Scoville Jenkins in the first two rounds.

But a resurgent James Blake awaited in the third round and took the match to the Spaniard. Having dropped below 200 in the world rankings after a trying year, Blake looked more like the Top 25 player everyone had been accustomed to seeing and aggressively took the match to Nadal. For his part, Nadal recovered to square the match at a set apiece when he broke Blake to end the second set, but Blake took advantage of sloppy play to win the third.

That took the starch out of Nadal, and Blake stormed to a four-set victory, winning 16 of the match's final 17 points.[3]

Nadal would finish the year with 11 titles, winning hardcourt tournaments in both China and his native Madrid around a pair of singles victories in Davis Cup play against Italy.[4] He pulled out of the season-ending Masters Cup due to a foot injury, but he did not let on just how serious the problem was until his autobiography years later.

"(The) diagnosis had initially been like a shot to the head," he recounted in 2011, with the injury revealed as a congenital bone problem. "The bone still hurts me. It remains under control, but we can never drop our guard."[5]

2006

Nadal's rehabilitation process to recover from the injury ruled him out of the Australian Open. His first tournament of the year was in France, where he reached the semifinals of the Marseille Open before losing to Arnaud Clement.[6] Still, Nadal had to be pleased because he told the Spanish paper Marca beforehand that "it would be a surprise to make the semifinals in Marseille on my return."[7]

His spirits were lifted further with a title in Dubai, rallying to defeat Federer in three sets in the final ahead of the two marquee hardcourt tournaments in the United States. But Nadal would again be stymied by Blake, this time in the semifinals at Indian Wells.[8] An ankle injury suffered there contributed to a surprising second-round exit in Key Biscayne against compatriot Carlos Moya, ending a 22-match winning streak against fellow Spaniards.

"For sure I didn't play 100 percent," he said after the match. "But he played very good, too. My physical condition is not my best now, especially after I turned my ankle. I have some problems when I play big points; when I go strong to one side. But that's not a special excuse."[9]

The three weeks between tournaments helped Nadal, as did returning to his favorite surface. He again bested Federer in a final, this time in four sets in Monte Carlo, and dropped one set in five matches en route to a title in Barcelona.[10] In Rome, he avenged his defeat to Moya in the first round and once more beat Federer in a clay-court final, though this would be the first of countless matches between the two.

After losing to Nadal in Roland Garros the year prior, Federer was determined not to let Nadal get into his head. But there was the 19-year-old, who had dealt the Swiss star his only two losses of the calendar year to this point. Federer took the first set by blanking Nadal in the tiebreak, but Nadal raised his play to win the next two sets. Federer, though, would answer the bell as well and not only took the fourth set but led 4-1 in the decisive fifth.[11]

Here, though, Nadal made his last stand as he defended his title. A misplayed lob from Federer gave the Mallorcan new life, and a service break put the match back on serve. But a double fault by Nadal gave Federer a pair of match points at 5-6, but he could not convert either of them. Federer took a 5-3 lead in the tiebreak, only to mishit a couple of forehands before Nadal took the final two points of the match on serve to end a marathon game that took nearly five hours.[12]

The clay-court scene then shifted to Roland Garros, where Nadal would be defending champion for the first time. He was seeded second to Federer, who was trying to become the first player since Rod Laver in 1969 to hold all four Grand Slam titles at once. Nadal breezed through his first two matches and had little resistance in the next two against Paul-Henri Mathieu and Lleyton Hewitt, getting pushed to four sets in those victories.[13]

In the quarterfinals, he won the first two sets against Novak Djokovic before the Serbian was forced to retire due to a bad back.[14] Nadal's clay-court win streak was now an unfathomable 58 matches, an Open Era record, and number 59 came with a semifinal victory against Ivan Ljubičić.

Once more it would be a final pitting Nadal and Federer, with the Swiss star carrying a weight the 20-year-old Nadal could not imagine at this point in his burgeoning career. Despite a 1-5 lifetime record against the Spaniard to this point, Federer looked comfortable and won the first five games of the match en route to an easy 6-1 first set.[15]

But for whatever reason, Federer could not sustain that level of play, and Nadal quickly raised his game. After squandering five break points in the first set, Nadal finally converted one to go up 2-0 in the second and leveled the match as quickly as Federer had taken the lead. The match then swung Nadal's way in the third set when he fought off three break points down love-40 to make it 2-all and then broke Federer the following game.[16]

Nadal then held Federer at bay the rest of the match, wrapping up a four-set victory via tiebreaker for his second straight French Open title and second Grand Slam, improving to 14-0 on the red clay of Paris.

"This is a fantastic victory and an incredible moment in my career as a tennis player," Nadal said. "Federer is the best player in history. No other player has ever had such quality."[17]

The switch to the grasscourt season provided some trouble for Nadal, who was forced to retire against Hewitt in the quarterfinals of the Queen's Club tournament due to a sore left shoulder.[18] He would get a week to recover, and entered Wimbledon as the number 2 seed to Federer.

It was almost déjà vu all over again in the second round as Nadal fell behind two sets to unknown American Robert Kendrick, ranked 237th in the world. Kendrick, who had never won a match on grass before his first-round win, flustered Nadal and forced a tiebreak in the third set by saving two set points on serve.[19]

There, Nadal finally found an opening and easily won the tiebreak to extend the match. He was two points from losing the match on serve at 4-5 in the fourth, but a forehand winner provided momentum and Kendrick faltered on serve the next game before Nadal forced a fifth set. And the Spaniard quickly took advantage of the tiring American, breaking him at love to start the set and serving out the match to overcome a major scare.[20]

Nadal's growing grasscourt confidence would be immediately put to the test in the third round against veteran American Andre Agassi, who was making his final appearance at the All-England club. Though seeded 25th and in the twilight of his career, Agassi was still a former Wimbledon champion, and at that point, one of only five players to have won a career Grand Slam.[21]

Still, Nadal was too good, powerful, and perhaps too young for the 36-year-old Agassi. He failed to concede a single break point to Agassi in blowing by the former champ in straight sets in barely more than two hours. The dominance that Nadal was building on clay was slowly expanding to his grass game, and his relentless ability to chase down shots harkening back to the days when Agassi was one of the best returners in the game.

"This was my best result on grass," Nadal said after the victory. "I'm improving, so I'm very happy for that. This Centre Court is the best."[22]

After routing Agassi, Nadal did likewise to surprise fourth-round opponent Irakli Labadze, and straight-set victories over Jarkko Nieminen and Marcos Baghdatis followed.[23] Nadal was in his second Grand Slam final of the year, and once more opposite Federer, who was seeking a fourth consecutive Wimbledon title and playing on his favorite surface.

At this point in his career, Federer was as dominant on grass as Nadal was on clay, carrying a 47-match win streak on the fast surface into the final.[24] Despite Nadal's 6-1 lead in the head-to-head matchup, this was the first time they had met on grass. Add the fact that Federer was 0-4 against Nadal and 55-0 versus everyone not named Nadal in 2006, and that meant the Swiss star would come in full guns blazing.

And it showed in the first set as Federer smoked Nadal 6-0. After not being broken in his previous four matches, Nadal dropped serve three times alone in the opening set, which took a mere 24 minutes.[25] Most opponents would have just bowed to Federer's greatness, but Nadal is not "most opponents."

He showed staying power by breaking Federer in the first game of the second set and had a chance to serve it out to even the match. But Nadal picked the absolute worst time to have a sloppy game, and Federer took full advantage as the Spaniard's double fault on set point made it two sets to love.[26]

Still, Nadal would not leave that quickly. He forced a fourth set by winning a tiebreaker, but any momentum he had was lost at 1-2 when he made an unforced error on a forehand that sailed long. Federer was able to regroup after that and fought off Nadal for his fourth straight Wimbledon title, but a message had been sent loud and clear after just two years in England: Nadal could most definitely win this tournament.

"This is his best surface, and I wasn't too far away, but he was better," Nadal defiantly said.[27]

Despite his solid showing at Wimbledon, there would be no titles for Nadal the rest of the year. He reached the quarterfinals of the U.S. Open before losing to Mikhail Youzhny in four sets as part of the Russian's surprising run to the semifinals. Nadal squandered three set points in the third set with the match knotted at a set apiece, and Youzhny overcame the nerves of his first quarterfinal appearance in a Grand Slam to upend the number 2 seed.[28]

Nadal capped his year at the Masters Cup in Shanghai where he lost to Federer in the semifinals of the eight-player tournament. But there was no shame in losing to Federer, who was at the apex of his career and won 92 of the 97 matches he played in 2006. The fact that Nadal had dealt him four of those five losses meant there was a budding rivalry, one that would carry on for more than a decade.[29]

2007

Nadal opted to start his preparations for the Australian Open in Chennai, India, where he reached the semifinals before losing to

Xavier Malisse.[30] He ventured onto Sydney, but he was forced to retire in the first set of his first match against Chris Guccione due to a thigh injury. It was a bit frustrating for Nadal, who could not pinpoint a time on when or how he suffered the injury.[31]

Entrenched as the world's number 2 player to Federer, Nadal was the second seed in Melbourne for the year's first Grand Slam. He did not take Kendrick lightly in the first round, easing by the American in straight sets. Nadal dropped one set in advancing to the fourth round where he faced Andy Murray, who by this point was an up-and-coming 19-year-old on the ATP Tour and ranked 16th in the world.[32]

The two played a classic match with wild momentum swings from both players as their games ebbed and flowed. Murray had the upper hand early thanks to his strong service game and some eagle eyes. He twice successfully challenged line calls with the Hawkeye to overturn points in his favor.[33]

He led 4-1 in the second set before Nadal flipped the script, winning eight of the next nine games to grab a 3-1 advantage in the third set. Now it was Murray's turn to counterpunch as he broke Nadal and eventually had the Spaniard on the ropes after winning the third set. Nadal, showed his veteran moxie if one can be called a veteran at age 20, fighting off five break points early in the fourth set before breaking Murray twice to force a winner-take-all fifth set.[34]

And that is just what Nadal did, finally solving the Scot's serve and cruising in the decisive set to reach the quarterfinals.[35] But that victory took a noticeable toll on the Spaniard as Nadal was comprehensively beaten in straight sets by Chile's Fernando Gonzalez. Opponents were starting to find flaws in Nadal's game outside of clay, most notably pushing him wide with their serves to neutralize his ability to track down shots relentlessly.[36]

Nadal failed to defend his title in Dubai, losing to Youzhny in the quarterfinals, but he regrouped in impressive fashion by winning at Indian Wells without dropping a set. The Mallorcan failed to do the American hardcourt double, though, falling to Djokovic in the quarterfinals in Miami.[37]

The clay-court season once more saw Nadal at his dominating best. He ripped through Monte Carlo without dropping a set, beating Federer in the final[38], and extending his win streak on that surface to 72 matches after capturing the title in Barcelona. He joined Mats Wilander as only the second player to win three straight titles in Barcelona, and it was his 20th ATP Tour title overall.

"To win another final, in Barcelona, at home here, it's a great feeling," he said. "The first time I won, it was like a dream, so what can I say, to win it for a third time, to win my 20th title here, it is an amazing feeling."[39]

That win streak reached 81 matches before Federer finally vexed his clay demons against Nadal with a three-set victory in the final at Hamburg. What made Nadal's loss so surprising was that he won the first set easily, and after failing to convert a couple of break points in the second, he dropped 12 of the final 14 games of the match to the Swiss maestro.[40]

It was the first time in six matches that Nadal lost to Federer on clay, and while Federer was eager to jump on any advantage he might have on the Spaniard ahead of the French Open, Nadal admitted that fatigue and a bad day was too much to overcome.

"I made more mistakes than usual, I played very short, and he feels the ball well," he said. "I can't be sad that I lose one match to the world's best player."[41]

For the second consecutive year, Nadal's defense of his title at Roland Garros was playing second fiddle to Federer's bid to hold all four Grand Slam titles simultaneously. If anything, though, it helped Nadal efficiently extend his perfect record in Paris. He was extended to a tiebreak just once in his six victories en route to the final and impressively dismantled Djokovic in the semis to earn another crack at Federer.[42]

It was clear Nadal wanted this win, not so much to avenge his loss to Federer in Hamburg, but to prevent history from happening at his expense. The first set was more about the Spaniard just surviving, as Federer threw everything he had at him early. All told, Nadal fought off ten break points in the opening set, drilling winners at every turn to thwart Federer.[43]

That took its toll on Federer, both psychologically and physically. As Nadal gained strength, Federer was having trouble keeping the ball in play. He wound up with 29 unforced errors on his forehand side and 59 in total, compared to the 27 Nadal made.[44] On that 59th error that handed Nadal to the match, he went to the ground and savored the moment, his eyes shut after realizing a third straight French Open title.

"Roger sometimes plays very, very aggressive, especially with the forehand," Nadal noted after the triumph. "But anyway, for me, he has the best forehand of the tour, no? But yes, the truth is he made some mistakes today, more than usual."[45]

There was no rest to be had as Nadal quickly made his way to England to tune up for Wimbledon, losing in the quarterfinals of the Queen's Club tournament before his appearance at the All-England club.[46]

Unlike the previous year when Nadal exceeded expectations on grass, his rivalry with Federer had now transcended surfaces. They were the two best players on the ATP Tour; to wit, Nadal had been ranked behind only Federer for 100 of the 177 weeks the Swiss star was atop the pecking order heading into this Wimbledon fortnight.[47]

But also unlike the previous year, Nadal had to scratch and claw almost every step of the way to get back to the final. He was pushed to five sets twice, first in the third round against Robin Söderling and the fourth versus Youzhny.[48] He eliminated Tomas Berdych in the quarterfinals and then caught a break in the semis when Djokovic was

31

forced to retire in the third set due to an infected blister on the small toe of his left foot.[49] Once more, Federer awaited in the finals.

And once more, the two rivals put on a show for the ages.

With nearly every Grand Slam final he reached, Federer was chasing history in some form or another. In this instance, he was trying to match the Open Era record of five straight Wimbledon titles won by Bjorn Borg.[50] Federer took the opening set in a tiebreak only to have Nadal use his punishing baseline game to grab the second.

Federer, though, used his crushing serve to forge an advantage in the third-set tiebreak to move within one set of the title. Nadal, as is the case so many times before, would not wilt. He broke Federer twice in the first three games of the fourth set and led 4-1 before needing a medical timeout to deal with some pain in his right knee.[51]

Nadal, though, would have the staying power to force a decisive fifth set. And he had both momentum and recent history on his side, having won his last seven five-set matches.[52] But both history and Federer would not be denied on this day. Nadal frittered away a pair of break points in Federer's first two service games, and the Swiss star summoned up his best shots of the match when he needed them, searing three forehand winners to break Nadal and go up 4-2.[53]

Federer would see out the game to extend his winning streak to 54 matches on grass and 34 on his personal playground of the All-

England club.[54] Nadal was inconsolable afterward, admitting he had cried for nearly a half-hour in the locker room following the loss.

"When I arrived at the locker room, I sat down, and as it's normal after losing the final of the tournament that you dream of winning, against the (world) number 1 and with lots of chances, I started to cry of anger, of sadness," he said. "When people started arriving, I sat down inside the tub. They were cheering me up.

"I thanked them, and I asked for being alone. I don't like people witnessing me crying."[55]

Nadal took out his frustrations on the field in Stuttgart, winning that tournament without dropping a set. He lost to Djokovic in the semifinals in Montreal to kick off the hardcourt season and was then forced to retire in the second round in Cincinnati against Juan Monaco due to a wrist injury and sore knee.[56]

"I didn't feel anything when I touched the racket," Nadal said. "I didn't have power in the legs. It was a strange feeling today."[57]

Those injuries would cause problems at the U.S. Open where he lost in the fourth round to fellow Spaniard David Ferrer in four sets. The match took 3 hours and 28 minutes, and a huge toll on the already-ailing Nadal, but he refused to let the injuries be an excuse for his defeat and praised Ferrer for his play.[58]

Nadal refused to take time off to heal, opting to play in the high-profile Masters Series tournaments. He lost in the quarterfinals in

Madrid and the finals in Paris, both to Argentine David Nalbandian, and Federer vanquished him once more in the semifinals of the season-ending Shanghai Masters.[59]

Even with the late-season struggles, Nadal still had a successful year with 70 match wins and six titles. But how long could he deal with the long shadow Federer was casting over him and the ATP Tour with his brilliance?

2008

For the second straight year, Nadal began his Australian Open tune-ups in Chennai. He reached the finals there, but after needing three sets and four hours to defeat his fellow Spaniard Carlos Moya, Youzhny administered one of the worst beatings of Nadal's professional career. Nadal took just one game from the Russian, who even conceded that he was given "a present from Rafa" due to the short turnaround.[60]

Nadal was once again seeded number 2 for the Australian Open and did not drop a set in reaching the semifinals opposite Jo-Wilfried Tsonga of France. Tsonga was a fringe Top 40 player on the tour with the athleticism to spare but had never put it together for a Grand Slam. The 22-year-old had his coming out party at Nadal's expense in Melbourne, routing the Spaniard in straight sets.[61]

It was one of those matches where anything Nadal did just did not matter because Tsonga was such a superior opponent that night. He even admitted it afterward, saying, "I tried to play slower, I tried to play faster, I tried to play more inside the court, more behind the baseline, but no chance. He played unbelievably."[62]

Nadal's title drought continued as he got progressively deeper in tournaments in Rotterdam, Dubai, Indian Wells, and Miami without winning it all.[63] But with the turning of spring comes the clay-court season, and it once more cured all of Nadal's ills. He stormed to another title in Monte Carlo, beating Federer in the final, and successfully defended his Barcelona title for a fourth straight year while avenging his U.S. Open loss to Ferrer in the final.[64]

He was upset by Juan Carlos Ferrero in the second round of the Rome Masters but regrouped to win the Hamburg Masters the following week with an impressive string of victories over Murray, Moya, Djokovic, and Federer.[65] It was the first time Nadal had won the German tournament, and he also served notice that he would again be a force to be dealt with at Roland Garros after improving to 8-1 versus Federer on clay.[66]

Nadal lived up to those expectations and more in winning his fourth straight French Open title. The Spaniard was dominant throughout his two weeks in Paris, becoming just the third player to win the tournament without dropping a set and needing a tiebreaker just once.[67]

His rout of Federer in the final was a master class in clay-court play. All of the pain and frustration Nadal harbored in losing the

Wimbledon final the previous year was unleashed on Federer, who was given no quarter on the red clay. The match took just 1 hour and 48 minutes, the shortest French Open final since Borg humbled Vitas Gerulaitis in 1980.[68]

It was also the first time Rafter lost a set 0-6 in a Grand Slam match since 1999, and the four games Nadal lost were the fewest in a final since Guillermo Vilas dropped three to Brian Gottfried in the 1977 final.[69] Even with Nadal wearing wraps on both knees, Federer provided barely any resistance as the Spaniard ran his perfect record at Roland Garros to 28-0.[70]

After such an emphatic dismantling of the world's top-ranked player, Nadal sustained that momentum across the English Channel by defeating Andy Roddick and Djokovic in the semifinals and finals of the Queen's Club tournament for his first title in England.[71]

Again, Nadal arrived at the all-England club as the number 2 seed to Federer, who again was chasing history in the form of an unprecedented sixth consecutive Wimbledon title to separate himself from Borg. Nadal dropped just one set in his first four victories and demolished Youzhny to reach the quarterfinals.[72]

In the round of eight, he would again square off against Murray, who carried a unique burden at this tournament as the player all of Britain would rally behind in hopes to see one of their own win the title. But Murray, who had to rally to get past Richard Gasquet in the previous round, was no match for Nadal as the Spaniard buried him and lost just 10 points on serve.[73]

While Rainer Schüttler pushed Nadal to a second-set tiebreak in the semifinals, it proved to be little more than a blip as the Mallorcan found his way back to Centre Court for a third straight final opposite the Swiss master. And the match between the two is what many widely consider the best game in the history of men's singles.

Heading into this tournament, there were finally some chinks in Federer's armor. Djokovic had finally broken through to win a major in Australia, the first time in 11 finals Federer had not reached the championship match, and while weakened with a bout of mononucleosis, Federer still tried to play his way into shape and had won only one title ahead of his fortnight in England.[74]

And there was still the scar tissue from Nadal's thrashing of Federer at Roland Garros. Lost in Federer's run to the final was that there were so many upsets he did not face a player in the top 20 before running into the Spanish buzzsaw.[75] So heading into this match, the difference between the two stars was negligible regardless of the difference in tour points that separated them in the rankings.

All the same, Federer carried a staggering 65-match winning streak on grass into this tournament as well as a 40-match run at Wimbledon. This was his domain, and he was master of it.

Nadal, though, would not bow. He broke Federer for an early 2-1 lead and fought off three break points before taking the first set.[76] The Swiss star wasn't rattled and finally converted a break early in the second set. But cool as you like, there as Nadal. The man from Majorca rallied to win the final five games of the second set, and all of a sudden, he was one set away from ending Federer's reign at the All-England club.[77]

But that would be a long time in waiting. Befitting his championship pedigree, Federer finally found his groove. Even an 81-minute rain delay was not enough to slow him down, winning the third set via tiebreak with four aces to extend the match.[78] The two stayed on serve throughout the fourth set, trading blows and points before once again needing a tiebreaker to determine the outcome.

This time, Nadal quickly gained the upper hand and was two points away from winning the title and was on serve. But a case of nerves gripped the Spaniard as he double-faulted and committed an unforced error, giving new life to Federer. Still, Nadal had two championship points later in the tiebreak, only to see Federer crack a service winner at 6-7 and then a stunning backhand passing shot at 7-8 after Nadal had pushed him wide with a forehand.[79]

Crisis averted. It was now down to one set, with no tiebreakers, with all the world to play for.

A second rain delay interrupted them at 2-all for nearly a half-hour, but they continued, battling each other as much as the impending darkness.[80] Nadal was finally getting to Federer's serve, forcing the Swiss star to fight back from love-30 in the 13th game. Two games later, on his third break point, Nadal finally got Federer to crack when he sent a forehand long.[81]

Once more, the championship was on Nadal's serve. And this time, he would not squander it. Federer again fought valiantly with a deft backhand on Nadal's third championship point, bringing the match back to deuce.[82] But Nadal's withering left-handed serve set up a fourth match point, and when Federer slapped a forehand into the net, 4 hours and 48 minutes after the first point, the Spaniard was finally a Grand Slam champion in a city other than Paris.

He rolled on the ground in delight, the flash bulbs of cameras catching the scene in the near-darkness of the All-England club. The king is dead, long live the king indeed.

"The most important thing is to win the title," Nadal said. "After that, you think about winning against the number 1, probably the best player in history or close, and the fact it was so dramatic. But it's one of the most powerful feelings I've had in my life."[83]

That summer continued to be a stellar one for Nadal, who won another Masters Series event in Canada and the Olympic gold medal in singles in Beijing. His straight-set win over Chile's Fernando Gonzalez vaulted him atop the ATP Tour rankings and ended Federer's reign of more than four years.

Despite the lofty accomplishments and the sustained effort to overtake Federer, Nadal seemed rather nonplussed about becoming king of the world.

"I may be number 1, but I played well last year, too," he said. "I was very happy being number 2. Probably, I'll be some time (again)."[84]

Armed with his new number 1 ranking, Nadal entered the U.S. Open as the top seed and eager to win a third consecutive Grand Slam. He played the part well early, rolling to straight-set victories in the first three rounds. Americans Sam Querrey and Mardy Fish extended him to four sets in the next two matches, but Nadal was two wins from a sixth Grand Slam title as he headed into the semifinals against Murray.[85]

Perhaps unburdened of the pressure of playing in front of his home fans, the 21-year-old Murray put together a sharp performance and took the first two sets. The match, though, was delayed by rain to the point it had to be pushed back to the next day. Nadal stirred thoughts of a rally as he won the third set and broke Murray early in the fourth after staving off seven break points for a 2-0 lead. But the Scot broke back to even the set at 3-all and eventually closed out the match on Nadal's serve with help from a net cord that allowed him to rifle a backhand passing shot on match point.[86]

It was the first time in six matches Nadal lost to Murray, and while the Scot would be denied his first Grand Slam title by Federer in the final, he was starting to elbow his way into the conversation as a potential winner, much like Djokovic had done before him.

"I'm disappointed, but at the same time I'm happy," Nadal said after the loss. "I leave the U.S. Open with positive memories. I go on the court all day with calm, try to fight as much as I can, go home knowing I tried everything.

"I had my chance in the fourth set. I just didn't come back," he added.[87]

Nadal bounced back from the disappointment of the U.S. Open by winning both his singles matches against Querrey and Roddick to propel Spain to the Davis Cup finals. His season, though, was cut short by injury at the Paris Masters as his thigh and knee injuries flared up again during the first set of his match against Nikolay Davydenko.[88]

While Nadal did not get to participate in Spain's Davis Cup final victory over Argentina, it was still a breakthrough year with his two Grand Slam titles and Olympic gold medal. He finished with an ATP Tour-leading eight wins and was named Player of the Year after compiling an 82-11 record while winning almost $6.7 million in prize money.[89]

2009

A new year meant a new place for Australian Open prep work as Nadal began his season in Doha, Qatar. There, he won two matches before losing to Gael Monfils in the quarterfinals in a tight 6-4, 6-4 defeat. Nadal, though, did team up with compatriot Marc Lopez to win the doubles title in straight sets over Daniel Nestor and Nenad Zimonjic.[90]

Nadal arrived in Melbourne as the top seed and quickly dispatched of his first four opponents, dropping just 28 games in those 12 sets.[91] He also outclassed number 6 seed Gilles Simon in straight sets in the quarterfinals before being put to an incredible test of stamina against fellow Spaniard Fernando Verdasco in the semis.

Verdasco was appearing in his first Grand Slam semifinal and had not beaten Nadal in six previous head-to-head matches. In fact, Nadal routed him in the French Open the past year, dropping just three games.[92] Both knew the prize awaiting in the final was a showdown with Federer, who had beaten Roddick the previous day and had his first chance to match Pete Sampras' all-time mark of 14 Grand Slam titles.[93]

Very little separated the two Spanish left-handers throughout the match. Verdasco won the first set in a tiebreak and had two set points in the second, only to see Nadal reel off four straight points and eventually level the match. The third set saw both players attack the other's serve, each recording two breaks before Nadal would blow through the tiebreak and have a chance to close out the match in four sets.[94]

Verdasco kept punching, though. He astutely took a medical timeout for treatment to deal with cramps and recovered sufficiently enough to force and win tiebreak to force a winner-take-all fifth as the clock passed midnight local time.[95] Nadal kept creating opportunities for himself to break Verdasco's serve in the fifth set, but he was unable to find that needed point for separation.

Verdasco had his chances as well, most notably in the ninth game up love-30 with everything to play for at 4-all. But here is where Grand Slam experience mattered, and Nadal had it in spades. He cracked off four straight points to keep the match on serve and pile the pressure on Verdasco. It came to a head in the next game as Nadal gave himself three match points. Verdasco erased two of them, but a double fault on the third ended the 5-hour, 14-minute marathon, the longest ever played at the Australian Open, as Nadal dropped to his knees and then laid on his back in delight.[96]

There was every reason to believe Nadal would be too tired to compete against Federer given the extra day of rest he had in addition to overpowering Roddick in his semifinal victory. Nadal offered no complaints about the Australian Open scheduling method after his semifinal win, content to just do what he needed to do to try and win a sixth Grand Slam title.

What the first set lacked in grace and fluidness it more than compensated for with tense play. Both Federer and Nadal were jittery early, and the Swiss man took a 4-2 lead as the two players combined for five breaks of service. Nadal eventually took the first set 7-5, and with it taking just under an hour to complete, fans at the Rod Laver Arena knew they were going to be in for the long haul.[97]

Despite fighting his serve the entire second set, Federer had enough to level the match. By this point, the cumulative fatigue of this match and his marathon semifinal victory were taking a toll on Nadal, who needed a thigh massage during a changeover in the third set.[98] He was clearly hanging on at this point, fending off six break points in a pair of service games to keep the set on serve. Nadal grabbed an advantage in the tiebreak with a jaw-dropping backhanded runner that unnerved Federer so much that he double-faulted on the next point to give the Spaniard the set.[99]

Federer found his bearings in the fourth set, but the serve that had brought him so much success in his rise to the pinnacle of the sport deserted him once more. Nadal trailed love-30 in the fourth game of the fifth set when Federer became unglued, hitting three unforced errors on the baseline and then a double fault.[100] Just like that, Nadal was up 3-1 and could run to daylight.

And he did. Federer fought off two match points trying to extend the contest, but when he sailed a forehand long to end the almost 10 hours of tennis Nadal played on consecutive nights, the Mallorcan became the first Spanish player to win a Grand Slam major on hardcourt as well as be the first Spaniard to triumph in Melbourne.[101]

The lasting memory of this title for Nadal is not him moving a step closer to completing a career Grand Slam, but instead, the classy sportsmanship shown by a champion to his esteemed and worthy adversary. To say that this loss devastated Federer is an understatement. He could barely compose himself during the trophy ceremony, and at one point, had to pull away from the microphone in tears as his voice cracked while saying, "God, it's killing me," he was so distraught.[102]

Nadal did not care that he improved to 13-6 lifetime against Federer or that he had beaten him in five of the seven Grand Slam finals they contested. It was one human being's compassion for another. Nadal stepped forward and wrapped his arm around Federer, giving the Swiss star time to compose himself to finish his conciliatory speech, which he did earnestly.

"I don't want to have the last word; this guy deserves it," Federer said. "So, Rafa, congratulations. You played incredible. You deserve it."[103]

The scene brought out a rare public introspection by Nadal as he addressed the crowd following his victory.

"It was an emotional moment, and I think it also lifts up sport, to see a great champion like Federer expressing his emotions," he said. "It shows his human side. But in these moments, when you see a rival who is also a comrade feeling like this, you enjoy the victory a little bit less."[104]

After a well-deserved week off, Nadal got back into the swing of things and reached the final in Rotterdam before losing to Murray. He bounced back quickly to win both his singles matches for Spain in a Davis Cup tie versus Serbia, ripping Djokovic in straight sets as his country advanced with a 4-1 win.[105]

He avenged his loss to Murray in the final at Indian Wells, but could not complete the American Masters Series double, losing to Juan Martin del Potro in three sets in the quarterfinals in Miami.[106] That gave way to Nadal's favorite time of year, spring on the clay courts, and he was in scintillating form as he racked up titles in Monte Carlo, Barcelona, and Rome, defeating Djokovic in the finals twice.

His win streak reached 19 matches before Federer surprisingly upended him in the finals in Madrid, though the fatigue of a three-set win over Djokovic in the semifinals may have contributed to Nadal's loss. That said, there was little separation between the two as Federer's two breaks of the Spaniard, one in each set, was enough for a victory.[107]

Once more, it was time for the French Open, and the spotlight was more squarely on Nadal as he sought a fifth consecutive title at Roland Garros. Yes, Federer was again trying to complete his career Grand Slam and match Sampras' all-time mark of 14 major titles, but the breakthrough 12 months Nadal had from his previous victory on the Parisian clay started to draw the inevitable questions about where the Spaniard could be among the all-time greats.

It was status quo in the first three rounds as Nadal ran his career French Open record to 31-0. He won all three matches in straight sets and looked lethal, yielding just five games to Australian Lleyton Hewitt in the third round. His next opponent would be Sweden's Robin Söderling, whom Nadal had routed 6-1, 6-0 in the third round in Italy and beaten at Wimbledon in five sets the previous summer.

It was the first time the Swede had reached the fourth round of a Grand Slam, and if he had any nervousness, it sure didn't show. If anything, that lopsided loss in Rome freed Söderling of any preconceived plans of how to beat Nadal and instead gave him the freedom to hit the ball with abandon and see what happens.

Nadal had no answer for all of the aggressive shots Söderling was unloading, especially on his serve. He broke the Spaniard five times in winning the first set 6-2, clearly flustering Nadal and preventing him from finding any rhythm.[108] It was the first time since the 2007 final that Nadal had dropped a set at Roland Garros.[109]

But he found a groove in the second set, getting an early break to go up 2-1 on Söderling. The Swede's strategy is finally coming into focus: he is hitting shots at Nadal's forehand to prevent the Spaniard from loading up his topspin-heavy backhand that is so effective on clay. The dry conditions are also helping Söderling because it makes his forehands that much faster. Still, Nadal is able to square the match by winning the second set in a tiebreaker.[110] Söderling continued to thrive on his risk-reward strategy of hard forehands, riding a break in the seventh game to a win in the third set. He is now one set away from pulling off one of the biggest upsets in French Open history, and Nadal is still searching for answers to get back into the match.

And in the fourth set, he nearly does. Nadal gets a quick break to go up 2-0, but Söderling breaks back stunningly to bring the match back on serve.[111] The other surprising thing at this point is that the crowd has now become decidedly pro-Söderling, in part to pull for the underdog but also recognizing the bigger picture that Nadal's loss would give Federer a clearer path to the title.

Nadal, though, continues to battle and he forges a 5-4 lead on serve. A golden opportunity to force a fifth set, however, comes and goes as he weakly puts a backhand on Söderling's second serve into the net. Instead of the game going 15-40 and having two break points, it's now 30-all, and Söderling has an escape route.[112]

To his credit, the Swede takes full advantage and forces a tiebreaker, which he wins emphatically 7-2 for the match. For the first time at Roland Garros, Rafael Nadal walked off the court as a loser in the French Open. His 31-match win streak snapped dramatically and shockingly, his bid to eclipse Borg with a fifth straight Coupe des Mousquetaires left in tatters by the world's 25th-ranked player.

"His game didn't surprise me; I was more surprised by mine," a stunned Nadal said. "It was my fault more than his. Well sure, he did well, he did very well. But I think I didn't play my best tennis."[113]

Söderling would continue his stunning run to the French Open final where he would lose to Federer as the Swiss legend completed his career Grand Slam and carved out his place in history by equaling Sampras with his 14th major title. There would obviously be more chances for Nadal to add to his six Grand Slam victories, but the next opportunity at Wimbledon would not be one of them.

Two days before the start of Wimbledon, Nadal announced he would not be able to defend his title due to tendinitis in his knees.[114] His relentless style of play, tracking down every shot, not conceding any point, and powerful baseline strokes had finally created enough cumulative damage that the 23-year-old was nowhere near 100 percent as he played.

"I've played with problems for the last two months. Unfortunately, I won't be able to play at Wimbledon. I'm just not 100 percent," he said in announcing his decision. "I'm better than what I was feeling a couple of weeks ago, but I just didn't feel ready to approach a tournament like this."[115]

Nadal would take a two-month hiatus from tournament play, making his return for the Masters Series in Montreal. He would reach the quarterfinals before losing to Del Potro, and then progressed to the semis in Cincinnati where he fell in straight sets to Djokovic.[116]

Between the time off and the lost points from being unable to defend his Wimbledon title, Nadal entered the U.S. Open as the number 3 seed behind Federer, who was trying to win his sixth consecutive title in New York, and Murray. The first three rounds went as well as they could have with Nadal dropping just one set total in those victories.

His first real challenge came from Monfils, a Frenchman with the athleticism to spare but also who had never had a compelling breakthrough to that upper tier of the ATP Tour in Grand Slam play. While some thought Nadal was trying to play through an abdominal injury suffered in his third-round win, the Spaniard shook off a slow start to record a four-set victory.[117] There was also a light-hearted moment at the end when a fan rushed onto the court to embrace Nadal before being taken away by security, but like most things, it did not faze the Mallorcan.[118]

Nadal moved within two victories of completing his career Grand Slam after knocking off Gonzalez in straight sets, but he ran into a buzz saw in the form of Del Potro. The Argentine played a near-flawless match in routing Nadal 6-2, 6-2, 6-2, and would eventually show the victory was no fluke by ending Federer's reign in Flushing Meadow in the final for his first Grand Slam title.[119]

There would be no other titles for Nadal in 2009 as he reached the semifinals in Beijing and Paris around a loss to Davydenko in the finals of the Shanghai Masters. He made a quick exit at the season-ending ATP Finals, losing in group play to Söderling, Davydenko, and Djokovic without winning a set.[120]

But if there was a silver lining to an otherwise trying year, it was lifting the Davis Cup trophy with his compatriots after Spain trounced the Czech Republic in the final. Nadal shook off a slow start to defeat Tomas Berdych in straight sets in the first singles match to set Spain on its way and won a dead rubber over Jan Hájek to complete the 5-0 whitewashing.[121]

"To finish the second half of the season with this ending is very important and nice, especially after all of the problems I had over those two months," said Nadal, referring to his injuries. "You have to be sure to enjoy these moments when they happen because you don't know when the next victory will come."[122]

2010

One of the things Nadal also said after the Davis Cup title was that he was not going to change his schedule much, which would bring in the question of just how much wear and tear his knees would be able to take over the course of the long season. Once more, his ATP season kicked off in Doha, where he was beaten in three sets by Davydenko in the final.[123]

Nadal entered Melbourne as the number 2 seed to Federer, who had by this point surpassed Sampras with his 15th Grand Slam title and was now in unprecedented territory by trying to further himself as the greatest of all time in the sport. For the first four rounds, things went mostly according to plan for Nadal as he advanced without much trouble or fanfare.[124]

It all went sideways against Murray, however. Both players were hitting the ball hard in the first set, but it went the Scot's way, 6-3. The second set was interrupted for a fireworks celebration that was taking place near Melbourne Park.[125] Nadal led the set 3-2 at that point, and both players retreated to the locker room to wait out the festivities. The Spaniard broke Murray in the first game after play resumed, but Murray broke right back.

Nadal fought off four break points at 5-5, only to see Murray blitz through the tiebreaker to go up two sets to none. Early in the third set, Nadal used a medical timeout to deal with some pain in his right knee, and the physical agony became too much to bear two games later when Nadal retired down 0-3 in the third set.[126]

An MRI that was taken after the tournament revealed a small tear in the back of Nadal's right knee. While the good news was that the injury was not a recurrence of the tendinitis, it did require at least a month's worth of rest and anti-inflammatory drugs.

"I feel good, and I am only thinking now of recovering well," Nadal said in a statement released through his agents. "My main goal right now is to get ready again and fit to play the upcoming events once I am able to compete. It's a big disappointment for me not to be able to play at Rotterdam this year."[127]

Nadal would wind up missing two months, making his return at Indian Wells in March. He showed little rust in reaching the semifinals before losing to Ljubičić in three sets in the semifinals, a process that he repeated in Miami where he lost to Roddick in the same round.[128]

The Mallorcan quickly and successfully transitioned to the clay-court season, winning the title in Monte Carlo without dropping a set. His decision to skip the Barcelona Open was justified with successes in Masters Series titles in both Rome and Madrid, defeating Federer in the final in his home country.[129] Nadal became the first player to sweep all three clay-court Masters Series events, and more importantly, served notice that he was heading to Roland Garros with confidence and momentum.[130]

Nadal was the number 2 seed for the French Open, and the Nadal of old was in full form as he cut through his half of the draw with relative ease. He did not face a tiebreak until his quarterfinal match against fellow Spaniard Nicolas Almagro, and the 19th seed put up a tough fight before bowing to Nadal in straight sets.[131]

While Nadal advanced, both Federer and Djokovic did not. Both stars were upset in the quarterfinals, Federer by Söderling and Djokovic by unheralded and 22nd-seed Austrian Jurgen Melzer, who would be Nadal's semifinal opponent. It was the first Grand Slam semi for Melzer, and while he had moments, he was not Nadal's caliber as the Spaniard returned to the French Open title for the fifth time for a chance to avenge his loss to Söderling in the final.[132]

Revenge was the last thing on Nadal's mind. He even admitted he was rooting for Berdych in the other semi-final since he had a better record against the Czech than he did versus the Swede.

"I never believe in revenge," Nadal said after his semifinal win. "I believe in trying my best in every moment. And if I lose, I lose, and congratulate Robin because he did better than me."[133]

Unlike last year, when Söderling went for broke and won points with every aggressive shot imaginable, Nadal kept his composure and returned fire in vintage form. He tracked down three sure-fire winners early in the contest to set the tone of the match, and this time it was the Swede who looked lost on the red clay as Nadal battered him point after point.

His knees were fine. The topspin-heavy backhand was excellent. The return of Söderling's booming serve was great. When the dust had finally settled, Nadal had committed only 16 unforced errors and emerged with a straight-set win and a fifth French Open title.

"I lost last year because I was not well-prepared, and I had very low morale last year, as well," said Nadal, who took back to the world's number 1 spot from Federer with the win. "But this time I'm back. I'm back – and I win."[134]

Nadal returned to the Queen's Club tournament for a Wimbledon tune-up and was bounced in the quarterfinals by compatriot Feliciano Lopez. Despite being the top-ranked player in the world, Nadal entered the All-England club as the number 2 seed to Federer, who had won the previous summer while the Spaniard sat out with a knee injury.

After a straight-set win over Kei Nishikori to open his tournament, Nadal was pushed to five sets in each of the next two rounds. He rallied from a set down to beat Robin Haase, ranked 151st in the world, dropping just three games in the final two sets.[135] He repeated the process against Germany's Philipp Petzschner, grinding through elbow and knee pain to advance to the fourth round.

"I am a little bit scared about the knee," Nadal admitted after the win. "I know my knees are not 100 percent recovered, but playing on clay and maybe on grass, if the matches are not very long, they can work well."[136]

Things returned to normal with a straight-set win in the quarters, but Söderling again loomed in the quarterfinals. Playing on Court 1 while Federer squared off versus Berdych on Centre Court, Nadal looked old, slow, and tired in the first set against the Swede. In fact, Söderling came within one point of blanking Nadal and eventually won the set 6-3.[137]

But while Federer was faltering, Nadal was persevering. A little bit of anger also helped. After Söderling correctly used video review to overturn a line call in the first game of the second set, Nadal was incensed that he lost the point as opposed to being it replayed. The

Spaniard reeled off the next six points to take control of the match and was never threatened in posting a four-set win.[137]

Next for Nadal would be Murray, who again bore the weight of Britain on his shoulders as they yearned for one of their own to be the first Wimbledon champion since Fred Perry did so in 1936. Nadal, though, ensured that they would be kept waiting for at least one year more. He grabbed the only break of the first set in the ninth game and then fought off two break points in the second before surviving a tense tiebreak to go up two sets to none.[138]

Murray did get a break to open the third set, but Nadal took the wind out of his sails by getting it back to make it 4-all and then closed out the match on the Scot's serve to make his fourth Wimbledon finals appearance.

"It was a very good match for me," Nadal said. "To beat Andy you have to play your best tennis. It's always a big challenge, and it was an amazing victory for me against one of the toughest opponents in the world."[139]

Nadal would face Berdych, who was making his first Grand Slam final appearance. The two opted for a baseline slugfest, and that almost always plays into the hands of the Spaniard. And that was the case here as Nadal efficiently dispatched of the Czech in straight sets for his second title at the All-England club and eighth career Grand Slam trophy.[140]

At the age of 24, he was already halfway in the chase to Federer's now all-time mark.

"It's more than a dream for me," Nadal said. "After a difficult year for me, missing the tournament last year, this year I came back and to have this trophy in my hands is more than a dream."[141]

Murray would gain a small measure of revenge in the semifinals of the Toronto Masters, and Nadal would only make the quarterfinals in Cincinnati as he prepared for the U.S. Open.[142] It was his second chance to complete a career Grand Slam, and this was as good a chance as any considering that Federer had failed to make the semifinals of the previous two majors.

Nadal was the number 1 seed and played the part convincingly, rolling into the finals without dropping a set. On the other side of the draw was Djokovic, who prevented yet another Rafa-Roger Grand Slam final by bouncing Federer in five sets in the other semifinal.[143]

It was the first time Nadal had reached the final in New York, and it was well worth the wait, regardless of who was on the other side of the net. The final was pushed back a day due to rain, and the rest helped both players as they were sharp early. Nadal, though, had the better of play in taking the first set. The two traded haymakers throughout the second set, which was interrupted at 4-all by a thunderstorm for two hours.[144] Djokovic squared the contest, but Nadal quickly reasserted himself thanks to a serve he had tinkered with before the tournament. An adjustment on his grip led to more velocity, and his service game now matched his already-punishing baseline game. The Spaniard won the final two sets, and at the age of 24, became the youngest player in the Open Era to complete the career Grand Slam and had won his third straight major.[145]

"For the first time in my career, I played a very, very good match at this tournament," said Nadal, not in a preening sense, but with one of self-satisfaction. "That's my feeling, no? I played my best match in the U.S. Open at the most important moment."[146]

Even Djokovic, who by now had created the third piece of the power triangle of men's tennis, gave Nadal his dues.

"He has the capabilities already now to be the best player ever," the Serbian noted. "I think (Nadal is) playing the best tennis that I've ever seen him play on hard courts. He has improved his serve drastically – the speed, the accuracy. And, of course, his baseline (game) is as good as ever."[147]

Nadal took a well-deserved two-week break before resurfacing in Bangkok to begin a tour of Asia. He lost in the semifinals there but captured a title in Tokyo with a straight-set win over Monfils. The Spaniard had a short tournament in Shanghai, losing to Melzer in the round of 16, but his standout campaign was more than enough to qualify for the season-ending ATP Finals in London.[148]

He rolled through his half of the eight-man group in round-robin play and then outlasted Murray in the semifinals for a long-awaited shot at

Federer in the final. While fatigued, he fell in three sets to the Swiss star, who warned Nadal he wasn't going anywhere anytime soon despite the Spaniard's strengthening hold on the world's number 1 spot with his victory.[149]

Nadal finished with an ATP Tour-high seven singles title that year and became the first man to win a Grand Slam title on clay, grass, and hardcourt in the same season. It also meant he would enter 2011 with a chance to complete the "Rafa Slam" and hold all four titles simultaneously.

2011

A new year meant another new start in Doha, which had picked up momentum as a season-opening tour spot because of its lucrative payout in both prize money and personal appearance fees. Nadal reached the semifinals of the Australian Open tune-up before losing in the semifinals to Davydenko.[150]

From Qatar, it was on to Melbourne, where now it would be Nadal with the chance to become the first player since Rod Laver in 1969 to hold all four Grand Slam titles. He did a good job through the first four rounds, showing little response to the building pressure as he cruised to victories without dropping a set.[151] But the dreams of completing this historic accomplishment quickly gave way to nightmares early in his quarterfinal match against Ferrer.

Early in the match, Nadal tweaked his hamstring. After the third game, he went into the locker room to receive treatment for the injury, but when he came back, the look of resignation on his face told the whole story.[152] For the second straight year, an injury on Australia Day in the quarterfinals of the year's first major would scuttle any dreams of a title.

To his credit, Nadal refused to retire, unlike the previous year against Murray. But he was obviously limited, unable to rush to the net for points, unable to load up on his preferred forehand, everything was physically taxing to the Mallorcan as his compatriot advanced to the semifinals at his expense in straight sets.

"I would prefer I don't talk a lot about the injury," he said. "I couldn't do more."[153]

He would take nearly a month off, returning to action to help Spain defeat Belgium in the first round of the Davis Cup by winning both his singles matches. But this year was quickly shaping up to be the year of Djokovic. The Serb beat Nadal in the finals at both Indian Wells and Miami, though he needed three sets to do so each time.[154]

Once more, Nadal would find his solace on the friendly clay surfaces of Europe, posting victories at Monte Carlo and Barcelona before again being struck down by Djokovic in the finals in Madrid. It ended a 37-match win streak on clay for Nadal and continued Djokovic's breathtaking start to 2011 in which he improved to 32-0.

"I came up against a great player obviously – he's having a monster year," Nadal conceded. "He was better; you have to accept that."[155]

The pattern repeated itself in Rome, where Djokovic emerged a 6-4, 6-4 winner in a 2-hour, 12-minute showdown of high-quality tennis. It was the fourth time in as many matches the Serb beat Nadal, but the Spaniard was optimistic ahead of Roland Garros, noting he "finished better than I started."[156]

Djokovic's all-consuming game made going to Roland Garros almost a relief for the rest of the ATP Tour since there would now be 127 other players gunning to hand the Serb his first loss of the year. Meanwhile, Nadal would be chasing his sixth French Open title and a 10th Grand Slam victory as the number 1 seed.

Nadal's title defense, though, was almost over before it began. A tough draw pitted him against hard-serving American John Isner in the first round. Isner, whose claim to fame in men's tennis will forever be his fifth-set 70-68 marathon win over Nicolas Mahut that took three days in the first round of Wimbledon in 2010, gave the Spaniard all he could handle.

Isner's serve proved to be problematic throughout the match, and he was up two sets to one after winning tiebreakers in the second and third sets.[157] Nadal, played a flawless fourth set, committing zero unforced errors, and gained a crucial break in the third game of the decisive fifth set to hold off the American in a four-hour slugfest.

"It was like a penalty shootout," Nadal said. "Isner's serve is almost unstoppable at the moment. In the tiebreak, you play under pressure all the time. It was a very, very tough opponent for me."[158]

Things returned to normal for Nadal as he swept his way to the final without dropping a set, beating Söderling in the quarterfinals and Murray in the semis. While everyone was expecting Djokovic to continue his reign of terror, it was Federer who turned back the clock with a vintage effort to deal the Serb his first loss of the season in the other semifinal.

So once more, it would be Rafa vs. Roger, who was looking for his first breakthrough against Nadal in the French Open final after three previous defeats. And in the first set, it looked like Federer had finally solved the clay-court conundrum that had plagued him against Nadal so many times before as he aced to a 5-2 lead.[159]

Nadal held serve to extend the set and then rallied with a flourish, he won the next seven games. Federer regrouped to force a second-set tiebreak, but by this point, Nadal was still feeling the match and took the second set as well. The Swiss star fought valiantly and eventually demanded a fourth set after breaking Nadal to go up 6-5 in the third.[160]

Nadal teetered ever so briefly but he held a break with two key forehand winners to go up 3-1, and the rest of the match was elementary. The Spaniard had successfully defended his title and joined Borg as the only six-time winners of the French Open. For

Nadal, it was also his 10th Grand Slam triumph, putting him alongside only six others in the history of the sport on the men's side.

"What a hard tournament this is to win," said an elated Nadal, "and what a special day it was. I want to congratulate Roger. I think we had a good match."[161]

The Mallorcan's Wimbledon tune-up at the Queen's Club ended with a loss to Tsonga in the quarterfinals, and he entered the All-England club as the number 1 seed. This time, however, his world's number 1 ranking would also be at stake because of Djokovic's superb season to date.

Nadal quickly extended his Wimbledon win streak to 17 matches with three straight-set wins. He finally encountered some resistance in the fourth round versus del Potro, and a foot injury early in his four-set win over the Argentine caused a great deal of concern.

"I thought I'd broken my foot, I felt terrible," Nadal said after a grinding match that lasted three and a half hours. "I sent for the trainer and didn't know if I'd have the chance to continue.[162]

The road would not get any easier as Nadal battled past both Mardy Fish and Murray in four sets in each of his next two matches. This time, Djokovic did not have to deal with Federer in a Grand Slam semi-final, Tsonga took out the Swiss legend the round prior, and the Serb was more than ready for the challenge.[163]

There will be few points in men's tennis where a player was on a level Djokovic enjoyed in 2011. He found separation in the first set by converting the lone break and then played an exquisite second set Nadal had no answers for. It was a 33-minute virtuoso performance in which Djokovic unleashed 13 winners to only two unforced errors.[164]

While Nadal would extend the match to a fourth set, there was never a moment that Djokovic was in fear of losing this contest. That was partially due to Nadal's erratic play, especially on his backhand side, but this was the Serb's moment. He was too good, too crisp, and after match point, the world's newly minted number 1 player in the world after beating the Spaniard.

"When one player beats you five times is because today my game don't bother him a lot," Nadal said. "Today, probably against me, he's playing better than my level. Find solutions, that's what I have to try, and that's what I'm going to try."[165]

Nadal would take off a month to recuperate, making his return for Masters Series events in Montreal (second-round loss) and Cincinnati (quarter-final defeat) ahead of the U.S. Open. He was the second seed behind Djokovic, but the draw also shook out in a way that Nadal would not meet Djokovic or Federer until the finals.[166]

Nadal played some scintillating tennis in New York, highlighted with a straight-set demolition of Roddick in the quarterfinals. While the American was dealing with both injuries and fatigue, the Spaniard showed little mercy in dispatching Roddick in under two hours. The final four of the U.S. Open was comprised of Djokovic, Nadal, Federer, and Murray, and for all intents and purposes, they could have been the only four in the 128-strong field.[167]

In the semifinals, Nadal took the match to Murray, who was beginning to feel the strain of the pressure of having to beat the other three to capture a first Grand Slam title. The difference of a break point converted by Nadal was enough for the first set, but Murray's inability to cash in three break points in the second before the Spaniard did so in successive games created a deficit too large to overcome.[168]

Murray did have a chance in the fourth set at 1-1, but he once more squandered a break point before Nadal crushed his will by breaking him for an unassailable 3-1 lead and eventually, a spot in the final opposite Djokovic.[169]

Djokovic's appearance in this final could partly be attributed to luck. Facing match point down 5-2 in the fifth set against Federer, he loaded up a forehand that could not have been placed more perfectly had he set the ball on the spot it landed. It unnerved Federer to the point that it swung the tone of the match and left the usually stoic Swiss star fuming.[170]

But it was a final that belonged to Nadal and Djokovic as the two set Flushing Meadow ablaze with breathtaking tennis. The Serb would try to frame a shot only to have Nadal hunt it down with alacrity, and the process would play itself out over and over and over until a point was earned, with emphasis on the word "earned."

Djokovic took the first set, but the match swung on the third game of the second. Nadal had just broken the Serb to level it at 1-all before the two threw everything they had at one another for the next 17 minutes. Nadal fought off five break points; there were eight deuces alone and a 28-shot rally that left Djokovic gasping for breath before Nadal finally cracked. He double faulted to set up a sixth break point and then netted a smash after a spectacular lob by Djokovic to extend the point.[171]

Even in losing the third set, Djokovic had done the unthinkable: He wore out Nadal, who could not keep up with the relentless pace the Serb was pushing. Djokovic took control of the fourth set with a break to go ahead 2-0, and with 55 winners to Nadal's 32, his magical year reached new heights by beating the Spaniard for the sixth time in as many matches in 2011.

"It was a tough match," Nadal conceded. "Physical, mental, everything. He's confident enough in every moment to keep believing in one more ball, one more ball."[172]

About the only thing that went right for Nadal the rest of the year was Spain's play in the Davis Cup. He defeated Gasquet and Tsonga in the semifinal win over France and repeated the trick against Juan Monaco and Del Potro in the final versus Argentina. It extended his winning streak in the international tournament to 16 matches as Spain successfully defended its title from 2010.[173]

"Today is one of the most emotional days of my career," Nadal said after winning the title for the third time overall. "After such a difficult year, this was a spectacular finale to the season. To win a final this way is very special."[174]

2012

Once more, Nadal could not get over the hump in Doha as he fell in the semifinals to Monfils in preparation for the Australian Open. After being the second seed to Federer for so many years, Nadal found himself behind Djokovic in the pecking order in Melbourne as he sought an 11th Grand Slam title.[175] The Spaniard was ruthless on the Australian hardcourts, rolling through his first four matches with ease.

The quarterfinal against Berdych, however, was a different story as the Czech took the first set and overcame a 5-2 deficit in the second before squandering a set point with a missed forehand. That gave Nadal a second life, and the Spaniard took full advantage, winning the tiebreak to square the match and powering through for a four-set win.[176]

The semifinals would pit Nadal against his old rival Federer, but it was also the first time since 2005 that the two were vying for a spot in a Grand Slam final as opposed to meeting in the final.[177] It was an intriguing contest because both of them struggled with the one part of their game that is their best: the forehand. Federer's forehand was wonky all night, and he committed a staggering 36 unforced errors with it.

Not that Nadal was much better by making 15 of his own. But the Spaniard did not feel his backhand was up to scratch in the contest and continued running around shots to set up his left-handed attack of choice.[178] For the third straight year, Nadal's match was interrupted by the fireworks of Australia Day, but this time the Mallorcan stayed injury-free and bossed Federer around the court.

He won a third-set tiebreak and would eventually win the match in four sets. While it took three hours and 42 minutes, it seemed to be a more mentally taxing match than a physical one given the string of mishits by both players. And for Nadal, it set up yet another final against Djokovic, the third straight time the two would meet in a Grand Slam final.

One of the fun aspects of being one of the best players of all-time is the ability to have matches considered among the best the sport has ever produced. Such was the case for Nadal in the 2007 Wimbledon final against Federer, and it would again be the case in Melbourne versus Djokovic.

Nadal came out swinging from the outset, determined to end his six-match losing streak to Djokovic. He grabbed a break for a 3-2 lead, only to have the Serb peg him back at 4-all. Nadal turned to his trusty forehand once more, this time gaining another break he consolidated to win the first set.[179]

But this was not going to be easy as Nadal double-faulted on set point to hand Djokovic the second set. The Serb threatened to run away with the match, breaking Nadal twice in the third set to move within one set of his third straight Grand Slam final win over the Spaniard.

Here, though, Nadal made a stand. Down 0-40 and 3-4 in the fourth, he successfully fought off three break points. The tiebreak went his way, ending a riveting 88-minute fourth set that created a one-set winner-take-all showdown.[180]

What made this all the more impressive was that Djokovic needed almost five hours to put Murray away in the previous round. Not that Nadal had been able to conserve a more significant amount of energy in defeating Federer. This final was now two champions at their zenith of shot-making, not backing down from the other and each looking for however slight an edge to forge a way to win.

And it almost belonged to Nadal, agonizingly so. He broke Djokovic to take a 4-2 lead in the fifth set, only to give the break away by fluffing a backhand. Just like that, the moment had passed for the Spaniard. Djokovic kept the match on serve to make it 4-all, then broke Nadal once more. Even Nadal winning a 32-shot rally to open the ninth game was not enough to slow down Djokovic. He broke the Spaniard again to gain a chance to serve out the match, and after fighting off one last break point from Nadal, he ended the longest match in Grand Slam history at 5 hours and 53 minutes with his third straight major title at 1:37 a.m. local time.[181]

Nadal tried to find a silver lining in being the first player to lose three consecutive Grand Slam finals, comparing it to his 2007 Wimbledon win over Federer. He noted, "I really understand that was a special match, and probably a match that's going to be in my mind not because I lost, no, because the way that we played."[182]

The Masters Series events in the U.S. were fruitless as he lost to Federer in the semifinals at Indian Wells and had to withdraw from a semi-final match against Murray in Miami due to a recurrence of the tendinitis in his right knee. It was one of those times where Nadal seemed to understand the short-term pain for the long-term gain, to keep himself fresh for the upcoming clay-court season in pursuit of a seventh French Open title.

"Today I have a really bad knee, and the last couple of days were tough for me," he said in explaining his decision. "But the positive thing is that the tendon has improved a lot in the last couple of years."[183]

The decision appeared to be wise, especially after finally beating Djokovic to claim a title in Monte Carlo. Nadal followed that up with another trophy in Barcelona, but Verdasco sent him home in the round of 16 in Madrid. He defeated Djokovic again, this time in the final in Rome as he served notice he was most certainly going to hunt out the Coupe des Mousquetaires trophy.[184]

But Nadal trying to pass Borg for the most French Open men's titles was not the dominant storyline in Paris. Instead, it was Djokovic seeking to become the first man since Rod Laver to hold all four Grand Slam titles simultaneously in what was being called the "Nole Slam." Nadal was second seed to Djokovic in Paris, and that seemed just fine as the Spaniard ripped through his first four matches by dropping just 19 games in those 12 sets.[185]

Almagro was the first to push Nadal to a tiebreak, but he swept by him and fellow Spaniard Ferrer in straight sets. Against Ferrer, he saved two break points in the fourth game and needed less than two hours to reach the final opposite Djokovic, who would mark his maiden French Open final appearance by trying to make history.[186]

Nadal raced out to an early 3-0 lead only to be pulled back in by Djokovic. But the Serb had trouble with his serve, and a double fault in the seventh game was enough separation to give Nadal the first set.[187] He added to Djokovic's misery in the second by breaking his serve on both sides of a 35-minute rain delay to push his advantage to two sets.

Djokovic finally found a semblance of consistency, ripping off six straight games to extend the match, but the rain proved to be more formidable than both players, forcing the match to be delayed until the next day.[188] The rain delay proved to be more fortuitous for Nadal than Djokovic, whose shot into the net shortly after the restart leveled the fourth set at 2-all. Eventually, Nadal's serve held true, and a record seventh French Open title was his after a four-set triumph.

"I was nervous last night, and I didn't feel ready to play until about three minutes before going out," Nadal admitted. "But I was much more aggressive today."[189]

Nadal opted to stay on the European continent for his Wimbledon tune-up, which was short-lived with a loss to Philipp Kohlschreiber in the quarterfinals of the Halle Open in Germany.[190] But his stay at the all-England club would also be a short one after a stunning five-set loss to Lukas Rosol in the second round.

Rosol had won just 18 ATP Tour matches in his career, but the 100th-ranked player in the world belied his underdog status with a stunningly brilliant performance that included 22 aces and 65 winners. Nadal was willing to concede that Rosol played well in the fifth set but also said he did not play well in the first three.[191]

While he did not offer any excuses about his ailing knees, it was taking a toll on Nadal. But it was still surprising that right before the start of the Olympics, which were going to be played at Wimbledon, Nadal announced he would not pursue a second gold medal because he was "not in condition" to compete.

In a statement, Nadal said it "is one of the saddest days of my career as one of my biggest ambitions that of being Spain's flag-bearer in the opening ceremony of the Games in London cannot be. You can imagine how difficult it was to take this decision."

What no one else also realized is that the injury was severe enough for Nadal to shut down for the rest of the year, forcing him to miss the U.S. Open.

2013

While Nadal used the last six months of 2012 to heal his knee sufficiently, it was a virus that ended his plans to participate in the first major of the New Year. He was forced to withdraw from an exhibition in Abu Dhabi because of the illness before deciding to skip the Australian Open as well.

"Because of the virus, I have been unable to get any match practice and simply would not be doing myself or my friends in Australia justice if I went down there so unprepared," he said in a statement to Australian Open officials. "It was a difficult decision, and I am extremely disappointed to be missing such a great event."[193]

Nadal would make his season debut in South America, losing in the finals of an indoor clay tournament in Chile before capturing the Sao Paulo Open in Brazil.[194] He was improving steadily with the level of competition, impressively beating Ferrer to win the Acapulco Open in Mexico. Nadal continued his winning ways at Indian Wells, besting Del Potro in the final for his 600th career victory.

"It's probably one of the most emotional victories of my career," Nadal said. "The support since I came back has been huge. It's an unforgettable week for me and an unforgettable tournament."[195]

Nadal continued his patient rebuild of his conditioning and took a month off before starting his clay-court season in Monte Carlo. There he lost in the finals to Djokovic, but rebounded to win his eighth career title in Barcelona and dropped one set in five victories to complete a Spanish double in Madrid.[196]

If anyone doubted Nadal was 100 percent, they only needed to see him wax Federer with ease in the finals of the Rome Masters, rolling to a 6-1, 6-3 victory to improve to 36-2 on the year. The victory took just 69 minutes, completing an impressive run that saw Nadal play 19 matches in 33 days.

"If anyone had told me (that) when I came back I would win six titles, I would have told them they were crazy. It has exceeded my wildest dreams," Nadal said.[197]

Both Murray and Del Potro were absent from Paris due to injury, which wound up putting Nadal and Djokovic in the same half of the draw at Roland Garros as the third and first seeds, respectively. That imminent collision course stayed on track as the two superstars dropped a combined three sets en route to their semifinal showdown.[198, 199]

Unlike their epic Australian Open final, this match was played in bursts. Clay requires more patience, something Nadal had acquired throughout his dominance at Roland Garros and something Djokovic was still learning to achieve. Nadal took the first set on the strength of a single break and had a chance to turn the match on its head after breaking the Serb again to take a 3-2 lead in the second, but Djokovic roared to life with four straight wins.[200]

The third set, however, belonged to Nadal with Djokovic taking just 12 points. Despite being broken twice in the fourth, Djokovic found the mettle to break back on each occasion, including at 5-6 with Nadal serving for the match. He won the tiebreak to force yet another all-or-nothing fifth set.[201]

Neither could create separation as the match stayed on serve to fray the nerves of players and fans alike. In the 14th game, Nadal stunned Djokovic by playing a shot between his legs for a point, but the Serb regrouped to keep the match going. Nadal held serve to go ahead 8-7, and Djokovic finally cratered with a series of errors in rapid-fire succession that shockingly gave the Mallorcan passage to his eighth French Open final.

"Serving for the match at 6-5 in the fourth, I was serving against the wind, so I knew it was going to be a difficult game. I was ready for the fight," Nadal said. "In Australia 2012, it was a similar match – today it was me (that won). That's the great thing about sport."[203]

The final would be an all-Spanish affair as Ferrer defeated Tsonga, who had beaten Federer in the quarterfinals. The final, though, would be as anticlimactic as Nadal's semifinal win over Djokovic was riveting. Nadal was painstakingly efficient in dispatching Ferrer in straight sets, becoming the first player to win a Grand Slam event eight times.[204]

Nadal improved to an eye-watering 59-1 lifetime at Roland Garros with his 12th Grand Slam title. He was now tied with Aussie great Roy Emerson for third on the all-time list, trailing only Federer and Sampras. Despite all the talk of history, Nadal opted to stay in the here and now as he was grateful his return from injury had resulted in a renaissance season to this point.

"I am a positive person, but there are doubts in this life," he said. "People who don't have doubts are so arrogant. Nothing is clear in this world. So for sure, I have doubts, but I work as hard as I could to be here. If I didn't, it's certain that I would not be back."[205]

In a nod to his knees, Nadal opted to bypass a warm-up tournament for Wimbledon and instead headed directly to SW19 to chase his third title at the All-England club. But that pursuit ended as quickly as it started with a straight-set loss to Belgian Steve Darcis, the 135th-ranked player in the world.

Nadal refused to make any excuses for his play, whether it was the lack of a tune-up on grass or his knees. Instead, he complimented Darcis for his play and that the Belgian "played a fantastic match."[206]

The disappointment of an early Wimbledon exit gave way to optimism for the U.S. Open after winning hardcourt titles in both Montreal and Cincinnati. Nadal beat Djokovic in the semis of the former and Federer in the quarters of the latter before surviving a barrage of aces against Isner in the finals in Ohio to win both sets via tiebreak.[207]

Nadal's climb back up the world rankings was almost complete as he entered the U.S. Open seeded second to Djokovic. His new-found confidence was on display throughout the early rounds as he did not drop a set until the fourth round, and even then, he eased past the 22nd-seeded Kohlschreiber in four sets.[208]

The Mallorcan ended the feel-good story of Spanish compatriot Tommy Robredo in the quarterfinals, losing just four games, and he made quick work of the Frenchman Gasquet in the semis to create another showdown with Djokovic to be the king of New York.

What this final lacked in length it compensated for with quality play. Nadal was the aggressor early with his forehand clicking to send Djokovic scurrying all over the court in winning the first set. Then it was the Serb's turn to find the range on his forehand as he leveled the match by taking the second.[209]

It appeared that Djokovic had grabbed the momentum of the match by its neck, surviving a 54-shot rally as he broke Nadal on three consecutive occasions en route to a 2-0 lead in set three. But Djokovic finally lost some steam and failed to capitalize on another break point, letting Nadal back into the match.[210]

The Spaniard rallied to draw level at 3-all, but another crucible came shortly after that as he faced three break points at 4-4. Nadal fought all of them off and then whipped a forehand on set point to break Djokovic, sapping the Serb of his resistance and moving within one set of victory.

There was one last point of defiance by Djokovic, but it was swallowed up in a sea of Nadal forehands as he emerged with a four-set victory for his second U.S. Open title and 13th Grand Slam victory, moving him four behind Sampras. People pondered whether he could track down the Swiss star who appeared to be heading into the twilight of his career.[211]

"Having this success is amazing," Nadal said after winning his 10th title of the year and improving to 22-0 on hardcourt surfaces for the season. "I never expected it. All my career I dreamed to be involved in matches like today. I enjoy every moment. I try my best, I have passion, and that's all I can do."[212]

While Nadal failed to add to his title haul, it was still a wildly successful year beyond anything he could have imagined when he set foot on that indoor clay court in Chile back in February. He was named ATP Tour Player of the Year, finished atop the rankings, and banked nearly $15 million in prize money.[213]

2014

Fully healthy at the start of a season for the first time in years, Nadal went back to Doha to kick off his prep work for the Australian Open. He finally emerged victorious in Qatar, fending off Monfils in three sets to claim the title.[214] In Melbourne, Nadal was now chasing history of his own as he had the chance to complete a second career Grand Slam and move into a tie with Sampras with his 14th major victory.

Nadal barely broke a sweat in the first three rounds, but an improved Nishikori, now seeded 16th, pushed him to a pair of tiebreakers around a 7-5 second set in a straight-set win.[215] Another up-and-comer awaited in the quarterfinals in Bulgarian Grigor Dimitrov. Nicknamed "Baby Fed" because his style of play was similar to Federer, the youngster proved to be worthy of the moniker as he pushed Nadal around with a punishing serve.[216]

The Spaniard had issues of his own with his service due to a blister that opened on his racket hand. He finally took advantage of the young Bulgarian's impatience in the third set tiebreak, fending off three set points before breaking Dimitrov twice in an eventual four-set win.[217]

Next up was the actual Federer, who had slipped to sixth in the rankings but still provided plenty of menace and bite. But in the grand scheme of this rivalry, this was a surprisingly one-sided semifinal as

Nadal advanced in straight sets to improve to 23-10 in the all-time series, including 9-2 in Grand Slam tournaments.[218]

In the bottom half of the draw, Djokovic had his 25-match win streak in Melbourne ended in the quarterfinals against Stan Wawrinka. While he may have been second to Federer in Switzerland, Wawrinka had quietly made a name for himself and had cracked the Top 10 of the ATP Tour rankings with consistently good tennis.

But his history against Nadal was anything but good. Wawrinka was 0-12 lifetime against Nadal, failing to win any of the 26 sets the two played.[219] It was also Wawrinka's first Grand Slam final. Surely he would still be no match for Nadal on the fast courts of Melbourne.

As the saying goes, that is why they play the game. Wawrinka used a lethal one-handed backhand as well as a big serve to keep Nadal on his heels. It did not hurt that Nadal injured his back early in the second half and required treatment to keep it loose, but still, this turned out to be Wawrinka's big night.

The burgeoning Swiss star took the match in four sets, marking the first time someone other than Nadal, Federer, Djokovic or Murray won a Grand Slam title since del Potro's stunning run to the 2009 U.S. Open title.[220] Once more, it looked like there needed to be more room made in the upper echelons of the ATP Tour.

"It has been a very emotional two weeks," Nadal said. "I'm sorry to finish this way. I tried very, very hard – this year was one of the more emotional tournaments in my career."[221]

Nadal would find solace in Brazil, winning a clay-court tournament in Rio de Janiero. He failed to win either of the Masters Series events in the U.S. and showed a surprising vulnerability in failing to win clay-court tournaments in his usual strongholds of Monte Carlo and Barcelona.[222]

He finally broke through in Madrid but lost to Djokovic in the finals in Rome.[223] All the same, everyone knew the road to the title at Roland Garros went through one man, and that was Rafael Nadal.

By this point in his career, it only became news if Nadal dropped a set in Paris. That did not happen until Ferrer grabbed the first one in the quarterfinals as the two played in blustery conditions. Undaunted, Nadal recovered and won 13 of the final 14 games to improve to 64-1 all-time at Roland Garros.[224] Next up was Murray, now a Wimbledon champion who was accustomed to the pressures that come with being a Grand Slam champion.

But Nadal swept him aside much like he does everyone else on Court Philippe Chartier, yielding just six games to the Scot in handing him his worst Grand Slam defeat ever. Nadal dropped just 10 points in his 12 service games and needed just an 1 hour and 40 minutes to advance.[225]

Once more, the last man standing in Paris opposite Nadal was Djokovic. The world's number 1 ranking was at stake as well as Nadal's shot at history to not only match Sampras, but also become the first male player to win five consecutive French Open titles.

Djokovic was again trying to complete his career Grand Slam and looked the better of the two early in winning the first set. Nadal gradually worked his way into the contest, taking full advantage of Djokovic's struggles in the second set to force a second-set tiebreaker at 5-6.[226]

The heat and humidity took their toll on both players, and they both struggled at different points as opposed to the superhuman levels they gave against each other at other Grand Slam tournaments. Additionally, the humidity helped Nadal more than Djokovic, as his topspin-heavy shots cut through the moist air.[227]

In the end, it was too much topspin and too much Nadal, who extended his record of French Open titles to nine, equaled Sampras' mark of 14, and closed within three of Federer. Additionally, he became the first men's player to win at least one Grand Slam title in ten consecutive years. Both exhausted players were effusive in their praise of the other, with Nadal telling Djokovic, "I'm sure you will win here in the future. I don't have any doubt about that."[228]

This time around, Nadal made the trip to Germany to tune up for Wimbledon, but that lasted all of one match as he lost to Dustin Brown in straight sets. At the All-England club, the Spaniard was seeded second but started out slowly in each of his early matches, dropping the first set before recording victories in each of the first three rounds.[229]

That pattern finally proved too much to overcome in the fourth round against Australian wildcard Nick Kyrgios, a teenager as talented as he is mercurial. On this day, however, the 19-year-old ranked 144th in the world was more talented than temperamental as he used a big serve to record 37 aces and send Nadal tumbling out of SW19.[230]

The year went from bad to worse for Nadal, who lost the world number 1 ranking when Djokovic captured the Wimbledon title and then suffered a wrist injury while practicing in Spain ahead of the hardcourt season.[231] It eventually precluded him from participating in the U.S. Open, but if anything, it was better than a recurrence of the knee injuries that had cut short most of his 2012 season.[232]

Eventually, Nadal would be sidelined three months before making his return to the tour in China. But after three tournaments and losses in three of seven matches, the Spaniard opted to pack it in for the year after a quarterfinal loss in Basel, Switzerland. However, the reason was not related to his wrist. It was his appendix. Nadal had revealed he was taking antibiotics to treat the ailment before going to Switzerland but said he was taking the rest of the year off.[233]

2015

It was back to the standard plan for Nadal, whose year started in Doha with a first-round loss to German Michael Berrer, ranked 127th in the world. He arrived in Melbourne seeded third behind Djokovic and Federer and needed more than three sets just once en route to the quarterfinals.[234] But much like the previous year when his mastery of Wawrinka ended after 12 wins, his hex over Berdych ended.

However, this was a far more emphatic loss as the Czech took out 17 frustrating losses by pounding Nadal in straight sets, winning 12 of the first 14 games and throwing a bagel in the second set for good measure.[235]

Nadal would retreat to his favored clay surface, winning his first title of 2015 by ripping through four Argentines in Buenos Aires. He was ousted in the quarterfinals at Indian Wells and the second round in Miami in the U.S. Masters Series, and the string of disappointments continued as he failed to extend his clay-court supremacy in previous strongholds Monte Carlo, Barcelona, Madrid, and Rome. In fact, he neglected to reach the finals in any of those events.[236]

Nadal's poor form coupled with his absence at the end of last year dropped him to a number 6 seed at Roland Garros as he sought a sixth consecutive title there and the "decima," his 10th overall on the red clay. Everything on the surface appeared normal through four rounds as Nadal worked his way through the field while dropping just one set.[237]

But the gulf in talent between contenders and pretenders closed up quicker this time as Nadal would have to get through Djokovic in the quarterfinals to extend his 39-match winning streak in Paris. And after all those years of heartbreak in which Nadal had denied first Federer and then Djokovic their dues on these red courts, the bill finally came against the Serb.

Djokovic was the aggressor throughout, the powerful shots emanating from his racket and not Nadal's. The Spaniard did not help himself with spotty play as he was still not the Nadal of his prime years. Still, Djokovic was primed for the occasion. He added a drop shot to his repertoire, mixing it in at opportune times to win the first four games of the match.[238]

Even when he battled back to win the next four games, it was evident that Nadal was not all there, both physically and mentally. Djokovic had finally slew the demons of his French Open past with a straight-set victory, though he would not complete his career Grand Slam on the court Nadal owns like no other in his sport until the following year. But at that very moment, there were doubts both on the outside and from Nadal himself.

"In the third, I am not happy about the way I tried," he said with stunning frankness. "It's not a big surprise, no? I didn't win enough before here. It's something that could happen when you see the draw. I lost in 2009, and it's not the end. I lost in 2015, and it's not the end. I hope to be back next year with another chance.

"There is only one sure thing. I want to work even harder to come back stronger."[239]

The loss served as a wake-up call of sorts as Nadal opted for more work ahead of Wimbledon. He was victorious in Stuttgart but lost in the first round at the Queen's Club. Nadal's struggles had dropped him to the 10th seed at the All-England club, and it was another stunningly quick exit for the Spaniard as he was bounced in four sets in the second round by German qualifier Dustin Brown.

It was a humbling departure for Nadal, who had now been shown the door at Wimbledon in four straight years by players ranked below 100 on the ATP Tour.[240] Making his Centre Court debut, Brown used a strong return game and aggressive serve-and-volley tactics to fluster Nadal to significant effect.

"Obviously this is a bad moment for me," Nadal said, still trying to process the defeat. "I have to keep going and working more than ever to try and change that dynamic. I am not happy, but I accept that I am not good enough."[241]

Nadal's season-long inconsistencies continued. He won a clay-court tournament in Hamburg, then failed to reach the semifinals in either U.S. Masters Series events ahead of the U.S. Open.[242] It was no better at Flushing Meadows where he shockingly capitulated a two-set lead and a 3-1 advantage in the third to Italian Fabio Fognini in the third round.

Despite a fifth set that lasted 52 minutes, there was a lack of confidence in Nadal, who watched Fognini fire 70 winners to his 30. He even admitted so after the match, noting, "What I (am) doing worse is playing worse than what I used to do the last couple of years. That's it."[243]

Nadal would finish the year with only three titles and a stunning 20 losses in 81 matches. Despite being ranked fifth in the world, it was clear at this point he was not a top-five player.

2016

If there was an answer to Nadal's struggles, it was not to be found on the other side of the world. He lost to Djokovic in the finals at Doha, then stunningly crashed out of the first round of the Australian Open against fellow Spaniard Fernando Verdasco. The two left-handers slugged it out for 4 hours and 40 minutes, but it was Verdasco who proved the better of the two, winning the final two sets to send Nadal to the first first-round exit of his career in Melbourne.[244]

Nadal finally found his confidence in Monte Carlo, where he beat Wawrinka, Murray, and Monfils in the final three rounds for his first title of the year. That sparked him to his ninth career title at Barcelona, though Murray and Djokovic would get the better of him in Madrid and Rome, respectively.[245] For the French Open, Nadal was the fourth seed, but it would be the first time a Grand Slam was played without Roger Federer, who was sidelined with a knee injury. The Spaniard asserted his usual dominance on clay early, winning both of his matches in straight sets and dropping just nine games in those contests.

But Nadal's bid for "the decima" would again be derailed, this time by a left wrist injury. He suffered the injury in the lead-up to the French Open and could no longer play through the pain ahead of this third-round match against Marcel Granollers.[246]

"Every day it was a little bit worse," Nadal said as he fought back the tears while explaining his withdrawal. "It's not broken, but if I keep playing (here) it's going to be broken. To win the tournament, I need five more matches... that is nearly 100 percent impossible."[247]

Nadal would take most of the summer off to heal, making his return at the Olympics in Brazil. Despite the layoff, the Spaniard was seeded third behind Djokovic and Murray. The chase of a second gold medal proved to be worth the wait as Nadal rolled through his first three matches and rallied to defeat local favorite Thomaz Bellucci in the quarterfinals. Later that day, he teamed with Marc Lopez to win the men's doubles gold medal.[248]

In a frenzied atmosphere in the semifinals, Nadal and Del Potro waged a fevered battle for a spot in the final. They split the first two sets before the Argentine finally broke through with a break in the ninth game of the third to go up 5-4. Backed by his South American fans, it was anything but a typical tennis match as they refused the chair judge's pleas for quiet.[249]

Nadal promptly broke back to send the Spanish faithful into cheers. Then it was Del Potro's turn, owning three break points to get within 6-5 and possibly serve for the match. Nadal would have none of it, slamming six straight points so that he could potentially break the Argentine for a crack at the gold medal.

Del Potro would hold his nerve and eventually force the tiebreak. But even that came with wild momentum swings as the Argentine went up 3-0 and then 5-2 before Nadal made one last charge to close within 6-5. He sent a forehand return long and was relegated to playing for the bronze.[250] But like most things for Nadal, that did not go his way either as he lost to Nishikori in three sets.[251]

Nadal's rough year would continue without a title, and he made a fourth-round exit at the U.S. Open in a five-set loss to Frenchman Lucas Pouille. By the end of the season, there was little fanfare for Nadal's quiet slide down the rankings as he ended the year ninth on the ATP Tour, the lowest he had been since July 2015.[252]

2017

Nadal opted to change things up ahead of the Australian Open, choosing to play his warm-up tournament in Brisbane. He played well, but squandering a break point up a set in his quarterfinal match against Milos Raonic proved to be his undoing as he lost in three sets to the Canadian.

From there, it was a short trip to Melbourne for the first major of the year. While Murray and Djokovic were the top two seeds, you had to scan further down to find Nadal at number 9, and further still to locate Federer, seeded 17th. Nadal's half of the draw almost immediately opened up when Djokovic was stunned in the second round by Denis Istomin.

After two easy victories, Nadal ran into his first challenge against number 24 seed and teenager Alexander Zverev, who was considered one of the best young players on the ATP Tour. The Spaniard battled to win the final two sets of the match, taking control in the fourth set by converting his third break point of a game tied 2-all.[253]

The road would not get any easier for Nadal as he faced the sixth-seeded Monfils for a spot in the quarterfinals. He kept the Frenchman at bay for two sets and then had to turn back a spirited challenge to win in four sets. It would mark the first time in almost two years that Nadal would be in a Grand Slam quarterfinal, and the whispers of the old guard's demise in Melbourne were starting to become slightly exaggerated.[254]

That is because, in the other half of the draw, Federer was also turning back the hands of time, though doing so was more surprising considering he was 35 years old. The Swiss legend had beaten a pair of Top 10 players to get to the last eight, first Berdych, and then a gritty five-setter over Nishikori.[255]

Nadal would get another crack at Raonic in the quarterfinals, and a tactical adjustment from the loss the previous week would come in handy. The Spaniard opted to move closer to the baseline to deal with Raonic's serve, which sometimes clocked 140 miles per hour, and he was able to get quick points on sharp-angled passing shots.[256]

He fought off six set points in the second set to frustrate Raonic and closed out the Canadian with a service break at love. With his 50th career win at Melbourne Park, Nadal was through to his first Grand Slam final since 2014, and the momentum for a throwback final against Federer grew as he did his part in beating Zvereva's brother Mischa in straight sets.[257]

To earn a date in the finals against Federer, who bested Wawrinka in the first semifinal, Nadal first had to go through "Baby Fed" as Dimitrov made his second appearance in a Grand Slam final four and first since Wimbledon in 2014. The Mallorcan was the aggressor early, winning the first set before Dimitrov began to find the range on his backhand to win the second and even the match.[258]

Nadal had a rare flash of temper in the third as he complained about a time violation he received from the chair umpire in the second set. Still, he bore down to win the set in a tiebreaker before Dimitrov responded in kind to set up a decisive fifth set. The decisive blow came in the ninth game when Nadal converted a break point as Dimitrov sent a forehand long. The Spaniard would close out the match on serve, ending a tense contest that lasted nearly five hours, and moved onto face Federer in a Grand Slam final for the ninth time in their storied careers.[259]

"To qualify for the final in a match like this means a lot to me," Nadal said courtside after the victory. "I never dreamed to be back in the final of the Australian Open in the second tournament of the year, after a lot of months without competing. But I am here now. I feel lucky. I feel very happy, really."[260]

There was a shared kinship spirit between the two old warriors for this match. Like Nadal, Federer had cut short his 2016 due to a knee injury, missing the final six months of the year to heal properly after admitting he came back too soon. The freak injury, suffered when running a bath for his children, seemed almost as odd as Nadal being unable to overcome the wrist injury that plagued him the previous year. When Federer went to visit Nadal to help him open an academy, the two could barely sustain a volley, let alone play Grand Slam-caliber tennis.[261]

Still, these war horses were going to meet head to head for the 35th time. There were no secrets left to uncover. The trips down Memory Lane were nice for Nadal, who noted that it "is exciting for me and for both of us that we still there and we still fighting for important events." But it also marked what could have been the last chance for the Spaniard to close the gap in Grand Slam titles on Federer and maybe overtake him.[262]

The first Grand Slam final between the two since Nadal won the 2011 French Open was, as expected, a cagey affair. Federer was making it a point to win points quickly since getting into a prolonged slugfest with Nadal would do him no favors, and the Spaniard was trying to keep him penned in a corner.

But Nadal struggled from the outset, spraying shots all over Melbourne Park. It came to a head in the seventh game when Federer converted a break point as Nadal sailed a backhand wide. That was enough separation for the Swiss man to take the first set.[263]

Nadal quickly regrouped and got his first break of the match to go up 2-0. A second followed soon after, and the string played out to let him even the match. Nadal had his chances in the first game of the third set, earning three break points, only to have Federer deny him each time with an ace.

Now, momentum was clearly on Federer's side as he broke Nadal twice in his next three service games and peppered the Spaniard with a service game that was ferociously on point. It went from 2-0 to 5-1 quickly, and Nadal suddenly found himself one set from defeat.[264]

But championship margins are often razor-thin, and such was the case as the two greatest players of their generation, and perhaps ever, continued to battle. Nadal found the slightest of creases in the fourth game, getting just his second break point in 11 tries, and it was enough to carry them into a pulsating fifth set.[265]

Nadal was poised to add to Federer's misery early in the fifth set. He watched Federer miss an inside-out forehand to grab an early break, then beat back the Swiss maestro on all three of his break points in the next game to go up 2-0.[266] So many times before, especially those times at Roland Garros, this would be where Federer would crack mentally, and Nadal would scatter the pieces of his psyche and add to his Grand Slam haul.

This time, however, things were different. Federer had made one critical tactical adjustment and concession for this final. He was returning shots on his backhand earlier in the bounce, preventing Nadal's unique top-spin heavy returns from getting so high that the returns to the Spaniard would lack power. The concession was that occasionally Federer would spray shots wide, but it also meant he was keeping Nadal off-balance and moving him on the baseline like a chess piece while also picking his spots to charge the net.[267]

After Federer took a medical timeout for a leg massage, he held serve to stay in the match. He had a chance to pull even, but Nadal saved a break point with a wicked cross-court and two-handed backhand winner before holding serve to make it 3-1.[268] Would that be enough to keep down Federer?

No.

Once more, Federer held serve. Nadal vaporized a break point with a fizzing forehand, but he was unable to hold serve as a backhand on game point clipped the net and fell wide. Federer gained a second break point and this time cashed in as Nadal's inside-out forehand sailed wide. The match was back on serve at 3-all, and it was all still to play for.[269]

Nadal continued to have issues dealing with Federer's serve, getting aced twice as the Swiss man went ahead 4-3. The problems snowballed quickly, and Nadal suddenly found himself down 0-40 and facing three break points. But he beat back each one, the last coming with an audacious high-kick second serve that handcuffed Federer to bring the game back to deuce.[270]

Federer won a 26-shot rally for another break point, Nadal again erased it. But the Spaniard could do nothing to save the fifth one, watching a filthy one-handed cross-court backhand from Federer land in. It was an all-time point from an all-time player. Now down 3-5, Nadal had to fight to extend the match.[271]

He almost got there, quickly grabbing a love-30 lead before Federer responded with an ace and forehand winner. Nadal survived one championship point, but on the second, Federer went to his old standby of a serve-and-volley with a forehand that appeared to nick the line. Nadal challenged the call for a video replay, and one of the most riveting finals between the two ended abruptly as the computer's simulated flight of the ball confirmed it had indeed, clipped the line.[272]

Ever gracious in defeat, Nadal was earnest in the post-match address to the crowd, saying, "Being honest, in these kind of matches, I won a lot of times against him. Today he beat me, and I just congratulate him. He did not surprise me. He was playing aggressively, and I understand that in a match against me."[273]

The run to the final provided a spark of sorts to both Nadal and Federer. The Spaniard reached the final of his next tournament, losing to Querrey in Acapulco, but it was Federer dealing him losses in the round of 16 in Indian Wells and the final of Miami.[274]

After a two-week break, Nadal looked like his usual self as the clay-court season kicked off. He won in Monte Carlo and Barcelona, the latter marking his 10th title in both cities. Another title in Madrid followed before Dominic Thiem, another of the next vanguard of players, beat him in the quarterfinals in Rome.[275]

That set the stage for Nadal's next attempt at his "decima," a record 10th French Open title. He would not have to worry about Federer, who was opting to scale back his tournament schedule to gear up for majors he felt he had a serious chance to contend in.

Nadal's surge in Melbourne and strong recent play pushed him to the number 4 seed behind Murray, Djokovic, and Wawrinka. And the Spaniard looked like the Nadal of old in the early rounds, dropping a mere 20 games in battering his first four opponents.[276] He advanced to the semifinals when compatriot Pablo Carreño Busta was forced to retire with an abdominal injury in the second set, but Nadal was also leading 6-2, 2-0 at that point.[277]

Another match against Thiem loomed in the semifinals, with the Austrian looking to top Nadal for the second time on his favored surface. But the "King of Clay" lived up this regal moniker, sweeping aside Thiem on the strength of six breaks as he attacked the youngster's backhand throughout a 6-3, 6-4, 6-0 win.[278]

The last obstacle between Nadal and his 15th Grand Slam title was Wawrinka, who had won the 2015 French Open and was in the final for the second time in three years. He was seeking a fourth Grand Slam title of his own after winning all three of his previous finals appearances.

Everything about the match was a throwback to Nadal's glory days, from the picture-perfect weather in Paris to his powerful baseline strokes to overwhelming an opponent, regardless of his quality. The Spaniard finished with only 12 unforced errors in a ruthless straight-set destruction that left Wawrinka so agitated that he smashed his racket after losing the second set.[279]

Nadal improved to 79-2 lifetime at Roland Garros, and only Bjorn Borg's 32 games dropped in 1978 were better than Nadal's 33. He finally moved past Sampras into sole possession of second place on the all-time majors win list and became the first player of the Open Era to win the same Grand Slam 10 times.[280]

"You need the right circumstances, the right ingredients, to win 10 French Open titles," Nadal said. "I don't know if I will ever meet the player who will do better than I did. It has been very special to me, and it's true that it is unprecedented. Trust me, I'm very happy I'm the one who did it."[281]

As the ATP Tour throwback era continued, it was onto Wimbledon to reunite with Federer at the All-England club. Nadal nearly pulled another magical moment out of his hat in the fourth round, rallying from two sets down before finally relenting 15-13 in the fifth set against Luxembourg's Giles Muller.

The deciding set alone took 2 hours and 15 minutes, longer than Federer's win over Dimitrov earlier that day. Nadal fought off two match points down 9-10 and held serve nine times to keep extending the match.[282]

Both Nadal and Federer will take part in the final major of the year at the U.S. Open. It is the only Grand Slam site where the two titans of their sport have never met in the final. With both Djokovic and Murray out due to injury, the draw shook out in such a way they would potentially meet in the semifinals. Though a trophy might not be at stake, rest assured there would be plenty of excitement if another match between the two would materialize.

Chapter 5: Nadal's All-Time Rivals

One of the things that make Nadal truly unique is that it is almost impossible to find any of his peers who have said a cross word about the Spaniard publicly. While Federer and Djokovic were tetchy at one point early in their respective careers, the warmth the Spaniard exudes as he plays tennis has resulted in most of his rivalries being relationships that feature mutual admiration and respect.

When they both decide to hang up their rackets, it will be somewhat odd to juxtapose Nadal's supremacy over Federer in the context of just how good Federer was overall. They are the two best players of their generation, and many former greats, including John McEnroe, have continually called Nadal and Federer the best.

But to own a 23-14 mark against the greatest player of all-time puts Nadal, having faced Federer in the final of a tournament 23 times, in a distinctive category. Consider how much further out of reach the Swiss maestro would be to anyone else on the ATP tour had he not beaten Federer in nine Grand Slam finals.[1]

In the 13-plus years that the two have faced each other on four different continents, there has always been an ebb and flow to them. Federer noticed in their first few matches starting with their initial meeting in 2004 that Nadal would be a force on the tour, revealing in a 2016 interview with Tennis Magazine "it was clear that the Spaniard would become the number one already in very competitive times."[2]

Matches between the two always had a certain ebb and flow. The grace Federer has on the court, the smooth agility, the all-around excellence, the lack of weakness in his game has always cut a sharp aesthetic contrast to Nadal, who looks and plays like every point is a match point he must save to extend the contest. It is no wonder Federer had to learn how to play Nadal mentally given the Spaniard's punishing nature from the baseline. To be able to tactically adjust at the age of 35 to make sure to remain competitive as Federer did in Melbourne, with repeated success in subsequent Masters Series events, is as much a testament to the Swiss star as it is Nadal's staggering consistency for more than a decade when healthy and otherwise.

Their recent resurgence is also a stirring testament to their staying power as much as it is a damning of the new generation that has yet to supplant them. Djokovic has been the closest to grabbing a foothold, capturing the "Nole Slam" in 2015-16, and Murray has had his moments when not crumbling under the weight of British expectations, either internal or external, but looking at the lists of former champions in each major in column-style is breathtaking.

From the 2004 Australian Open until 2012 Wimbledon, Nadal and Federer combined for 27 of the 35 Grand Slam titles. Djokovic was the only player to win more than one in that span, and his second major did not come until the 2011 Australian Open. They had a stranglehold on the sport, and unique to Nadal, he was lord and master of Roland Garros. He still is with only two losses in 81 matches there.

If not for Nadal, it can be argued Federer could have reeled off 11 straight Grand Slam titles and captured two calendar-year Slams. If that had happened, there would not be any arguments about who the greatest of all-time was. The Spaniard willed himself into the conversation through his dominance on clay, and then learned how to win on different surfaces to challenge Federer and make a debate of the "GOAT."

What is somewhat amusing is that Federer's current four-match winning streak over Nadal also stands as the longest of his career against the Spaniard.[3] While people were already pointing to that potential U.S. Open semifinal matchup, Nadal admitted he would prefer "an easier" opponent while understanding the public want.

"I know you want to hear the other way, that I would love to play with him," Nadal said in a press conference ahead of 2017's last major. "No, of course, I understand that's going to be great for our history. It's true that we played in all Grand Slam finals ... it sounds very good, but the real thing, I prefer to play against another player – an easier one, if it's possible."[4]

The two of them, though, continue to be more concerned with adding to their respective legacies than worrying about who will win the next match between them. But Nadal continued his glass half-full routine when asked about the surprising success the two have enjoyed this year.

"In January, yes," Nadal admitted when asked if their success was unexpected. "Now, a little bit less. Of course, it's something that probably you and we didn't expect, to have that much success, but here we are. And we worked well, we worked with passion, and we played well. So let's see how we finish the season."[5]

One of the byproducts of having faced Federer in so many finals is that Nadal had to beat someone good to get there. Enter the second rival of tennis' "Big 4," Novak Djokovic. The Serb has a razor-thin 26-24 edge in the all-time series, but Nadal has won four of the six times the two have vied for a Grand Slam title.[6]

Djokovic, though, does have one of the two rarest types of victories over Nadal, his straight-set quarterfinal victory in the 2015 French Open. In looking at the stats of that match, what stood out was Djokovic's ability to take full advantage of Nadal's second serve. The Serb won 23 of 37 points on Nadal's second serve, which helped him earn 18 break point chances. His seven converted were two more than Nadal had attempts.[7]

The two have met at all four Grand Slam venues, with Nadal owning a 9-4 record in those matches. Until the Spaniard beat him in Madrid earlier this year, however, Djokovic had gained the upper hand in the rivalry by winning 11 of the previous 12 clashes between the two.[8] The Serb has also been very complimentary to Nadal concerning the growth of his career, noting "the rivalry with Rafa is very special. When I started to be a stronger player, I had to find ways to win, especially against Rafa and Federer. Until a few years, I didn't know if I could dominate because they were there."[9]

Nadal has gotten the better of Murray often, winning 17 of the 24 matches between the two. The Spaniard won the first six matches between the two, so Murray has been more competitive in the last ten years.[10] Like Djokovic, they have faced each other at all four majors, with Nadal owning a 7-2 edge in those matchups. None of them, though, have come in a Grand Slam final.[11]

And while it necessarily does not constitute a "rivalry" in the traditional sense, Nadal has manhandled most of his compatriots with relative ease. Against current Spanish players ranked in the Top 200 on the ATP Tour as of Aug. 28, 2017, Nadal is a cumulative 89-15 mark. He has faced Ferrer the most, winning 24 of the 30 contests between the two.[12]

Chapter 6: Rafael Nadal's Personal Life

For as accessible as Rafael Nadal is concerning assessing his play in a match or talking about tennis, he is inversely shy about divulging details of his personal life. Many fans and tennis followers know of the strong bond he has with his uncle and coach Toni, but not much beyond that. There have never been too many people of note in his entourage.

The Daily Telegraph serialized parts of his 2011 autobiography, which revealed his close familial relationships, including the strain he endured in 2009 when he learned that his parents were going to separate after one of the biggest triumphs of his life at the Australian Open while flying from Melbourne to Dubai.

"The news left me stunned. I didn't talk to my father on the rest of the trip home. My parents were the pillar of my life, and that pillar had crumbled. The continuity I so valued in my life had been cut in half, and the emotional order I depend on had been dealt a shocking blow."[1]

One of the things that passage also revealed was just how structured Nadal kept his personal life, which was a stark contrast to what appeared to be a happy-go-lucky player on the court who wore bright sleeveless shirts that showed off sinewy arms and somehow made capri pants fashionable for men with his success. Those bright colors hid a dark secret that he kept well-hidden.

"Our whole world was destabilized, and contact between members of my family became, for the first time that I had been aware of, awkward and unnatural; no one knew at first how to react.

"My attitude was bad. I was depressed; lacking in enthusiasm. On the surface, I remained a tennis-playing automaton, but the man inside had lost all love of life. ... I became a different person, distant and cold; short and sharp in conversation. They (team members) worried about me, and they worried about the impact of my parents' separation on my game."[2]

His play bears out his phrase of being a "tennis-playing automaton." In the tournaments immediately after he learned of his parents' separation, he reached the finals of a tournament in Rotterdam, won both his singles matches in a Davis Cup tie versus Serbia, won at Indian Wells, and reached the quarterfinals in Miami.[3] Nadal was dominant in the clay-court season leading up to the French Open, losing only to Federer in the finals in Madrid after wins in Monte Carlo and Rome.[4] It was easy to write off the loss, even one that ended a 33-match win streak on clay, partially due to the four-hour win over Djokovic the round before.

His clipped answers in the post-match interview room offered few clues to his mental state. Consider some of his responses:

"There are no positives; there is little to analyze. He broke and broke, and I went home."[5]

"To me, this tournament has nothing to do with Paris. This tournament is practically another surface compared to Paris."[6]

"He was simply better than me. It doesn't help to play four hours yesterday."[7]

He hid the physical toll all these matches were taking on him, most notably his feet and knees. Clay does no favors for a man, especially given Nadal's punishing style of play. His mind became a dam of sorts for his body. How much pain could he withstand before he would come undone? It did not matter that Nadal was the greatest player the world had ever seen on clay, chasing his fifth straight French Open. Every player has a breaking point.

Every human has a breaking point.

Nadal's came with that stunning four-set loss to Söderling in the round of 16 of Roland Garros. He knew his game wasn't up to snuff in this particular match, and he also noted afterward the crowd did not support him when his supremacy was finally challenged in Paris.[8] Two years later, the truth finally came out in that autobiography as he came undone.

"Maybe I should not have competed at Roland Garros, but I had won the championship the previous four years, and I felt a duty to defend my crown, however unlikely the prospect of victory felt. Sure enough, I lost in the fourth round to Robin Söderling, of Sweden, my first ever defeat in that tournament.

"This finally pushed me over the edge. I'd made a huge effort to be in shape for Roland Garros, battling to overcome both my parents' separation and the pain in my knees, but now I knew that, debilitated in mind and body, I could no longer keep going."[9]

The good news for both Nadal and his parents was that there was a happy ending. Ana Maria and Sebastian reconciled in 2011, and they appeared together in the Royal Box at Wimbledon that summer. About two months before Nadal's autobiography came out, Tennis.com writer Peter Bodo made an astute observation on the potential impact of the separation had given Rafael Nadal. He said that he was "an obedient son who's never questioned the impermeability of the familial cocoon, and how losing dominion over a patch of earth where he has known only spectacular success might affect a young and not still fully formed tennis player."[10]

Right now, Rafael Nadal is still married to tennis. One tends to forget he just turned 31 in June, and if Federer is any indication, he still may have plenty of miles left on the playing odometer and more Grand Slam titles to be won. His single-mindedness has put tennis front and center in his life despite enjoying a long-term relationship with Maria Francesca Perello.

If Nadal is the antithesis to Federer on the court, then Perello is the antithesis to Federer's wife Mirka as well. Also a native of Majorca, the 28-year-old has opted for a life outside of tennis. In fact, pictures of the girl nicknamed "Xisca" were few and far between until last year, and any quotes from her regarding her relationship with Nadal were scarce.

As part of The Daily Telegraph's blowout of Nadal's autobiography in 2011, she seemed content to stay out of his way, and in turn, create a life of her own.[11] Perello has little use for the fanfare and limelight, something that is occasionally hard to avoid when every year the British tabloids cover the social scene of Wimbledon with as much fervor as they do the actual matches played at the All-England club. And she also values each of their independence.

"Traveling together everywhere, even if I could, would not be good either for him or for me," she said in a 2011 interview. "He needs his space when he is competing, and just the idea of me hanging around waiting on his needs all day wears me out. It would asphyxiate me. And then he would have to be worrying about me … If I followed him everywhere, I think there's a risk we might stop getting together."[12]

While they may seem standoffish, it does appear that Nadal is in it for the long haul with Perello. They knew each other before they started dating more than ten years ago, and Nadal has admitted he can see a life together, complete with children. But it also appears that the traditional upbringing Nadal had with his parents in which they were constantly around is also one he wants to have for his potential family.

"I am quite a family person, my education has been towards family," he said in an interview with the Spanish paper La Nacion. "You never know what will happen in the future, but I understand that I will form a family, have kids, I do not know how much. I love children, but one does not decide unilaterally, it takes two. I would like to have more children, but I cannot say whether two, three, or four."[13]

Both of Nadal's parents are trustees in his charity foundation, with his mother serving as president. Perello is part of a three-woman team that handles the day-to-day operations of the RafaNadal Foundation and is listed as the Projects Director on the website's home page.[14] The charity, which will turn ten next year, tries to help socially disadvantaged youth through sport and education. As part of its mission, it cites "the values we consider of greatest importance for the personal growth of each one of our beneficiaries: exertion, respect, friendship, equality, and confidence."[15]

According to the most recent annual report available from 2015, the charity claims to have helped more than 700 children in both Spain and India where it has an education center in Anantapur.[16]

Chapter 7: Rafael Nadal's Legacy

Let us start with the obvious: Rafael Nadal is the best player to have ever played on a clay-court surface in the history of tennis. To win ten tournaments on any surface means a player had, at worst, a decent career on the ATP Tour. To win ten tournaments on one surface means a player could be labeled a specialist on a given surface.

To win 10 Grand Slam tournaments over the course of a career puts a player in the conversation to be among the best players in tennis history. To win 10 Grand Slams at one tournament means that player's dominance is unrivaled. Now take that one step further, and remember Nadal also has won ten times at both Monte Carlo and Barcelona in addition to the ten important ones at Roland Garros, and you have a recipe for success unparalleled in the Open Era.

And the Monte Carlo Masters is not some rinky-dink tournament. It is among the 1,000 Masters Series events, which the respective tours consider a notch below a Grand Slam and a vital tune-up for the French Open. It's part of an overall dominance on the slower surface in which he has won 91.7 percent of the 424 matches he's skidded along the clay while playing.[1] There have been only 35 occasions he has lost when playing on clay, which makes those two defeats in 83 matches in Paris all the more amazing.

But Nadal evolved into something more than a clay-court specialist. The combination of a tireless work ethic from both player and coach created something special. Nadal challenged and often played better than a rival many will consider the greatest player in the history of men's tennis. He has won nearly two-thirds of his matches against Federer, who has a lifetime winning percentage of 81.8 percent heading into the U.S. Open.[2]

Here is an even better way of looking at it: almost 10 percent of Federer's 245 losses have come to Nadal.[3] And the Spaniard has nearly as close of a record against Djokovic (24-26) as Federer does (22-23).[4] Nadal's brilliance came by way of tenacity, of learning and applying his craft, how to repeatedly exploit the one chink in his opponent's armor to gain unique success. While it admittedly does not take much to move Federer emotionally, few players drove him to emotional despair with their play like Nadal did.

Being one of eight players to complete a career Grand Slam, and being one of the dominant players in an era in which three accomplished the feat puts Nadal in a unique light. While he will likely wind up finishing behind Federer for the most career Grand Slams, his status as the youngest player to accomplish the career slam in the Open Era likely will remain for decades to come. That is partly because Nadal helped make sure the current crop of rising stars would never find the same levels of success he, Federer, and Djokovic enjoyed.

A good player can win on multiple surfaces and winning the U.S. and Australian Opens are going to be part of Nadal's legacy, though he is running out of opportunities in Melbourne to complete a second career Slam. It is the fact that he won Wimbledon twice, the first time at the absolute apex of Federer's career, and again two years later, that people will cite as "Exhibit B" after the 10 French Open titles when they make the argument for Rafael Nadal as the best player in men's tennis. That, like Federer, he was more than a one-trick pony, even if his style often could be viewed as such.

Detractors will argue that Nadal helped usher in the power game of tennis because he was content to try and outslug everyone from the baseline regardless of surface. Why would you change something that works just because of aesthetics, especially in something as competitive as men's tennis? Nadal's greatest asset was his unique style of hitting the ball. He generated so much power and topspin that opponents often could not catch up. It took Federer almost 15 years of playing Nadal to come up with a method to level the playing surface, so to speak, and even he admitted it is sometimes a haphazard way to play against Nadal because of the concession of a certain amount of points because of mishitting the ball.

By passing Sampras for second on the all-time Grand Slam wins list, Nadal also cemented that his era with Federer, Djokovic, and Murray will be considered the best era of men's tennis in the Open Era. Did McEnroe, Connors, and Borg have more personality? Maybe. But each of the four aforementioned greats we get the privilege of watching now definitely have their unique styles. From Federer's grace to Nadal's "Vamos!" and fist pumps to Djokovic's feistiness to

Murray's running dialogue with himself, there is no lack of on-court entertainment in this edition of men's tennis even if it is top heavy.

In the end, Nadal has provided the perfect foil to Federer's greatness with his own. He is the grit to Federer's polish, the unorthodox to Federer's classic. They are a curious yin and yang who have blazed a trail that at some point, the next generation will finally grab hold of and chase in both titles and stature. But at the end of the day, Rafael Nadal has always been true to himself, win or lose, though it is always easier when you win more than you lose.

"The glory is being happy. The glory is not winning here or winning there. The glory is enjoying practicing, enjoy every day, enjoy working hard, trying to be a better player than before."[5]

Every day Nadal did that, he became that better player. And as a result, he is one of the best there ever will be.

Final Word/About the Author

I was born and raised in Norwalk, Connecticut. Growing up, I could often be found spending many nights watching basketball, soccer, and football matches with my father in the family living room. I love sports and everything that sports can embody. I believe that sports are one of most genuine forms of competition, heart, and determination. I write my works to learn more about influential athletes in the hopes that from my writing, you the reader can walk away inspired to put in an equal if not greater amount of hard work and perseverance to pursue your goals. If you enjoyed *Rafael Nadal: The Inspiring Story of One of Tennis' Greatest Legends,* please leave a review! Also, you can read more of my works on *Roger Federer, Novak Djokovic, Andrew Luck, Rob Gronkowski, Brett Favre, Calvin Johnson, Drew Brees, J.J. Watt, Colin Kaepernick, Aaron Rodgers, Peyton Manning, Tom Brady, Russell Wilson, Michael Jordan, LeBron James, Kyrie Irving, Klay Thompson, Stephen Curry, Kevin Durant, Russell Westbrook, Anthony Davis, Chris Paul, Blake Griffin, Kobe Bryant, Joakim Noah, Scottie Pippen, Carmelo Anthony, Kevin Love, Grant Hill, Tracy McGrady, Vince Carter, Patrick Ewing, Karl Malone, Tony Parker, Allen Iverson, Hakeem Olajuwon, Reggie Miller, Michael Carter-Williams, John Wall, James Harden, Tim Duncan, Steve Nash, Draymond Green, Kawhi Leonard, Dwyane Wade, Ray Allen, Pau Gasol, Dirk Nowitzki, Jimmy Butler, Paul Pierce, Manu Ginobili, Pete Maravich, Larry Bird, Kyle Lowry, Jason Kidd, David Robinson, LaMarcus Aldridge, Derrick Rose, Paul George, Kevin*

Garnett, Chris Paul, Marc Gasol, Yao Ming, Al Horford, Amar'e Stoudemire, DeMar DeRozan, Isaiah Thomas, Kemba Walker and Chris Bosh in the Kindle Store. If you love tennis, check out my website at claytongeoffreys.com to join my exclusive list where I let you know about my latest books and give you lots of goodies.

Like what you read? Please leave a review!

I write because I love sharing the stories of influential athletes like Rafael Nadal with fantastic readers like you. My readers inspire me to write more so please do not hesitate to let me know what you thought by leaving a review! If you love books on life, tennis, or productivity, check out my website at claytongeoffreys.com to join my exclusive list where I let you know about my latest books. Aside from being the first to hear about my latest releases, you can also download a free copy of *33 Life Lessons: Success Principles, Career Advice & Habits of Successful People*. See you there!

Clayton

References

Chapter 1 Bibliography

1. "Rafael Nadal biography." The Famous People. Web.
2. "About Manacor." abcMallorca. Web.
3. Ibid.
4. Meese, Phillip. "Forgotten Idols: Miguel Angel Nadal." 22 February 2016. Last Word on Sports. Web.
5. Ibid.
6. Ibid.
7. Almond, Elliott. "South Koreans wear down Spain for a tie." 18 June 1994. Los Angeles Times. Web.
8. Yannis, Alex. "Italy Soars Aboard the Baggio Express." 10 July 1994. The New York Ties. Web.
9. Baldridge, Martin. "Rafael Nadal: The Making of a Champion, Part 1, Chapter 1." 25 June 2012. Bleacher Report. Web.
10. Ibid.
11. Ibid.
12. Ibid.
13. Baldridge, Martin. "Rafael Nadal: The Making of a Champion, Part 1, Chapter 2." 25 June 2012. Bleacher Report. Web.
14. Ibid.
15. Ibid.
16. Ibid.
17. Baldridge, Martin. "Rafael Nadal: The Making of a Champion, Part 1, Chapter 3." 25 June 2012. Bleacher Report. Web.
18. Baldridge, Martin. "Rafael Nadal: The Making of a Champion, Part 1, Chapter 4." 25 June 2012. Bleacher Report. Web.
19. Ibid.
20. Ibid.

Chapter 2 Bibliography

1. Baldridge, Martin. "Rafael Nadal: The Making of a Champion, Part 2, Chapter 1." 20 July 2012. Bleacher Report. Web.
2. "Rafael Nadal 2001 Bio." ATP Tour. Web.
3. Ibid.

4. Ibid.
5. "The Junior Championships, Wimbledon. ITF Tennis. Web.
6. Ibid.
7. Ibid.
8. "Rafael Nadal 2002 Bio." ATP Tour. Web.
9. Baldridge, Martin. "Rafael Nadal: The Making of a Champion, Part 2, Chapter 2." 20 July 2012. Bleacher Report. Web.
10. Raj, Prakhar. "Rafael Nadal: Rafa's Wimbledon Journey and Popcorn." 16 June 2011. Bleacher Report. Web.
11. "Rafael Nadal 2003 Bio." ATP Tour. Web.
12. "Rafael Nadal 2004 Bio." ATP Tour. Web.
13. Ibid.
14. "Hewitt survives test against Nadal." 24 January 2004. CNN via Reuters. Web.
15. "Rafael Nadal 2004 Bio." ATP Tour. Web.
16. "Prodigy Nadal Shocks Federer at ATP Miami Masters Series." 30 March 2004. Tennis-x. Web.
17. Ilic, Jovica. "Rafael Nadal wins first ATP Title in Sopot." 15 August 2017. Tennis World USA. Web.
18. Garber, Greg. "Beginning of a rivalry? Roddick strikes first." 3 September 2004. ESPN. Web.
19. Clarey, Christopher. "Nadal Defeats Roddick at Davis Cup." 3 December 2004. The New York Times. Web.
20. "Brave Hewitt battles past Nadal." 24 January 2005. BBC Sport. Web.

Chapter 3 Bibliography

1. "Rafael Nadal Player Ranking History." ATP Tour. Web.
2. "Rafael Nadal 2005 Bio." ATP Tour. Web.
3. Ibid.
4. Ibid.
5. "Nadal Defeats Coria in Epic Rome Final." 9 May 2005. Tennis-X. Web.
6. McCarvel, Nick. "Rewind: Rafael Nadal's first French Open title in 2005." 1 June 2015. USA Today. Web.
7. Ibid.

8. "Rafael Nadal vs. Xavier Malisse." 25 May 2005. Tennis Live. Web.
9. "Rafael Nadal 2005 Bio." ATP Tour. Web.
10. Hodgkinson, Mark. "Nadal unruffled by agent provocateur." 31 May 2005. The Daily Telegraph. Web.
11. Ibid.
12. Ibid.
13. "Rafael Nadal 2005 Bio." ATP Tour. Web.
14. Bierley, Stephen. "Nadal beats Federer in battle of wills." 3 June 2005. The Guardian. Web.
15. Ibid.
16. "Teenager Nadal knocks out Federer." 3 June 2005. BBC Sport. Web.
17. Ibid.
18. Ibid.
19. "Teen Nadal gives Spain reign over French Open." 5 June 2005. USA Today. Web.
20. Ibid.
21. Ibid.
22. Bierley, Stephen. "Battling Nadal brings the king to his feet." 5 June 2005. The Guardian. Web.

Chapter 4 Bibliography

1. "Rafael Nadal 2005 Bio." ATP Tour. Web.
2. Ibid.
3. Clarke, Liz. "Blake Stuns number 2 Nadal in Four Sets." 4 September 2005. The Washington Post. Web.
4. "Rafael Nadal 2005 Bio." ATP Tour. Web.
5. "Rafael Nadal admits pondering switch to golf after 2005 injury." 22 August 2011. The Guardian via The Associated Press. Web.
6. "Rafael Nadal 2006 Bio." ATP Tour. Web.
7. "Nadal: I won't be at my peak." 1 February 2006. EuroSport via Reuters. Web.
8. "Rafael Nadal 2006 Bio." ATP Tour. Web.
9. "Moya Snaps Nadal 22-Match Spanish Win Streak in Miami." 25 March 2006. Tennis-X. Web.
10. "Rafael Nadal 2006 Bio." ATP Tour. Web.

11. Allen, Ja. "When in Rome: Roger Federer vs. Rafael Nadal 2006 Rome Masters Final." 26 April 2010. Bleacher Report. Web.
12. Ibid.
13. "Rafael Nadal 2006 Bio." ATP Tour. Web.
14. Bierley, Steve. "Weary Nadal gains respite from Djokovic retirement." 7 June 2006. The Guardian. Web.
15. "Nadal ends Federer dream in Paris." 11 June 2006. BBC Sport. Web.
16. Ibid.
17. Ibid.
18. "Shoulder Forces Nadal to Quit London Match." 17 June 2006. The New York Times. Web.
19. "Nadal survives scare to set up tie with Agassi." 29 June 2006. The Guardian. Web.
20. Ibid.
21. Newbery, Piers. "Agassi bows out to ruthless Nadal." 1 July 2006. BBC Sport. Web.
22. Ibid.
23. "Rafael Nadal 2006 Bio." ATP Tour. Web.
24. "Nadal's green feet." 8 July 2006. EuroSport. Web.
25. Clarey, Christopher. "Federer Defends Turf for Fourth Wimbledon Title." 10 July 2006. The New York Times. Web.
26. Ibid.
27. Ibid.
28. "Youzhny beats Nadal in New York." 6 September 2006. BBC Sport. Web.
29. "Roger Federer 2006 Bio." ATP Tour. Web.
30. "Rafael Nadal 2007 Bio." ATP Tour. Web.
31. "Guccione through after Nadal Retires." 9 January 2007. ABC.net. Web.
32. "Rafael Nadal 2007 Bio." ATP Tour. Web.
33. Harlow, Phil. "Valiant Murray succumbs to Nadal." 22 January 2007. BBC Sport. Web.
34. Ibid.
35. Ibid.
36. Bierley, Steve. "Wild man of Santiago keeps his head and sends Nadal hurtling out." 24 January 2007. The Guardian. Web.
37. "Rafael Nadal 2007 Bio." ATP Tour. Web.

38. Ibid.
39. "Nadal cruises to third title." 29 April 2007. Eurosport via Reuters. Web.
40. "Federer ends Nadal's clay streak." 20 May 2007. BBC Sport. Web.
41. Ibid.
42. "Rafael Nadal 2007 Bio." ATP Tour. Web.
43. Macur, Juliet. "Nadal Defeats Federer for French Open Title." 11 June 2007. The New York Times. Web.
44. Ibid.
45. Ibid.
46. "Rafael Nadal 2007 Bio." ATP Tour. Web.
47. Macur, Juliet. "Nadal Defeats Federer for French Open Title." 11 June 2007. The New York Times. Web.
48. "Rafael Nadal 2007 Bio." ATP Tour. Web.
49. Oxley, Sonia. "Nadal reaches final after Djokovic retires." 7 July 2007. Reuters. Web.
50. "Federer matches Borg record." 8 July 2007. The Guardian. Web.
51. Ibid.
52. Ibid.
53. Ibid.
54. Ibid.
55. Schlink, Leo. "The day Roger Federer made Rafael Nadal cry." 26 December 2007. The Herald Sun. Web.
56. Kinney, Terry. "Nadal Retires from Cincinnati Masters." 15 August 2007. The Washington Post via The Associated Press. Web.
57. Ibid.
58. Robbins, Liz. "Ferrer Ousts Nadal from U.S. Open." 5 September 2007. The New York Times. Web.
59. "Rafael Nadal 2007 Bio." ATP Tour. Web.
60. Ananthanarayanan, N. "Tired Nadal routed by Youzhny in Chennai final." 6 January 2008. Reuters. Web.
61. Dickson, Mike. "Unseeded Tsonga blows away Nadal to reach Australian Open final." 24 January 2008. Daily Mail. Web.
62. Ibid.
63. "Rafael Nadal 2008 Bio." ATP Tour. Web.
64. Ibid.

65. Ibid.
66. Rogers, Iain. "Nadal gains revenge over Federer in Hamburg." 18 May 2008. Reuters. Web.
67. "Rafael Nadal 2008 Bio." ATP Tour. Web.
68. Hodgkinson, Mark. "Roger Federer curshed by Rafael Nadal at Roland Garros." 9 June 2008. The Telegraph. Web.
69. Ibid.
70. Ibid.
71. "Rafael Nadal 2008 Bio." ATP Tour. Web.
72. Ibid.
73. Cheese, Caroline. "Brutal Nadal sweeps aside Murray." 2 July 2008. BBC Sport. Web.
74. Martin, Dave. "Reliving Wimbledon 2008 Final: The Greatest Match Ever." 30 August 2015. Epoch Times. Web.
75. Ibid.
76. Ibid.
77. Ibid.
78. Clarey, Christopher. "Nadal Ends Federer's Reign at Wimbledon." 7 July 2008. The New York Times. Web.
79. Ibid.
80. Martin, Dave. "Reliving Wimbledon 2008 Final: The Greatest Match Ever." 30 August 2015. Epoch Times. Web.
81. Ibid.
82. Ibid.
83. Clarey, Christopher. "Nadal Ends Federer's Reign at Wimbledon." 7 July 2008. The New York Times. Web.
84. Nichols, Peter. "Nadal strikes precious gold and wakes up on top of the world." 17 August 2008. The Guardian. Web.
85. "Rafael Nadal 2008 Bio." ATP Tour. Web.
86. Newbery, Piers. "Murray stuns Nadal to reach final." 7 September 2008. BBC Sport. Web.
87. Ibid.
88. Pretot, Julien. "Federer and Nadal pull out injured in Paris." 31 October 2008. Reuters. Web.
89. "Rafael Nadal 2008 Bio." ATP Tour. Web.
90. "Rafael Nadal 2009 Bio." ATP Tour. Web.
91. Ibid.

92. "Revisiting the Nadal vs Verdasco 2009 Australian Open semi-final epic." 16 January 2016. Roar. Web.

93. Clarey, Christopher. "Nadal Survives to Face Federer." 30 January 2009. The New York Times. Web.

94. "Revisiting the Nadal vs Verdasco 2009 Australian Open semi-final epic." 16 January 2016. Roar. Web.

95. Ibid.

96. Clarey, Christopher. "Nadal Survives to Face Federer." 30 January 2009. The New York Times. Web.

97. Bierley, Steve. "Nadal wins battle for place in history by edging past Federer in Melbourne." 1 February 2009. The Guardian. Web.

98. Ibid.

99. Ibid.

100.   Clarey, Christopher. "Nadal Defeats a Tearful Federer in Australia." 1 February 2009. The New York Times. Web.

101.   Ibid.

102.   Ibid.

103.   Ibid.

104.   Ibid.

105.   "Rafael Nadal 2009 Bio." ATP Tour. Web.

106.   Ibid.

107.   "Federer Wins Madrid Open; Defeating a Run-Down Nadal." 17 May 2009. The New York Times via The Associated Press. Web.

108.   Eckstein, Jeremy. "Rafael Nadal: A Look Back at his 2009 French Open Loss to Robin Soderling." 5 May 2013. Bleacher Report. Web.

109.   Clarey, Christopher. "Nadal is Stunned, Losing Where He Feels Most at Home." 31 May 2009. The New York Times. Web.

110.   Eckstein, Jeremy. "Rafael Nadal: A Look Back at his 2009 French Open Loss to Robin Soderling." 5 May 2013. Bleacher Report. Web.

111.   Ibid.

112.   Ibid.

113.   Clarey, Christopher. "Nadal is Stunned, Losing Where He Feels Most at Home." 31 May 2009. The New York Times. Web.

114.   Stafford, Mikey. "Rafael Nadal's knee problem 'may force him to end his career early.'" 27 June 2009. The Guardian. Web.

115.   Hodgkinson, Mark. "Defending champion Rafael Nadal pulls out because of injury." 19 June 2009. The Daily Telegraph. Web.

116.   "Rafael Nadal 2009 Bio." ATP Tour. Web.

117.   "Rafael Nadal returns to world number 2 spot with Gael Monfils win." 9 September 2009. The Daily Telegraph. Web.

118.   Ibid.

119.   Donegan, Lawrence. "Juan Martin del Potro crushes Rafael Nadal to meet Roger Federer in final." 13 September 2009. The Guardian. Web.

120.   "Rafael Nadal 2009 Bio." ATP Tour. Web.

121.   Bierley, Steve. "Spain seize 2-0 lead in Davis Cup final." 4 December 2009. The Guardian. Web.

122.   "Rafael Nadal: Season-ending Davis Cup win crucial as he plans for 2010." 6 December 2009. The Daily Telegraph. Web.

123.   "Rafael Nadal 2010 Bio." ATP Tour. Web.

124.   Ibid.

125.   Hodgkinson, Mark. "Andy Murray reaches last four as Rafael Nadal retires." 26 January 2010. The Daily Telegraph. Web.

126.   Ibid.

127.   "Nadal out for month with injured knee." 29 January 2010. ESPN via The Associated Press. Web.

128.   "Rafael Nadal 2010 Bio." ATP Tour. Web.

129.   Cambers, Simon. "Rafael Nadal beats Roger Federer to win Madrid Masters." 16 May 2010. The Guardian. Web.

130.   Ibid.

131.   "Rafael Nadal 2010 Bio." ATP Tour. Web.

132.   Branch, John. "Nadal to Face Soderling in an Intriguing Final." 4 June 2010. The New York Times. Web.

133.   Ibid.

134.   "Nadal wins fifth French Open title." 7 June 2010. ESPN via The Associated Press. Web.

135.   "Rafael Nadal survives scare to dispatch Robin Haase." 24 June 2010. The Daily Telegraph. Web.

136.   Bull, Andy. Rafael Nadal avoids defeat in five-setter against outsider." 26 June 2010. The Guardian. Web.

137.   Reason, Mark. "Rafael Nadal shrugs off nightmare start to oust Robin Soderling." 30 June 2010. The Daily Telegraph. Web.
138.   Newbery, Piers. "Rafael Nadal beats Andy Murray in semi." 2 July 2010. BBC Sport. Web.
139.   Ibid.
140.   Newbery, Piers. "Rafael Nadal beats Berdych in final." 4 July 2010. BBC Sport. Web.
141.   Ibid.
142.   "Rafael Nadal 2010 Bio." ATP Tour. Web.
143.   Ibid.
144.   "Rafael Nadal completes career Grand Slam." 14 September 2010. ESPN via The Associated Press. Web.
145.   Ibid.
146.   Ibid.
147.   Ibid.
148.   "Rafael Nadal 2010 Bio." ATP Tour. Web.
149.   Mitchell, Kevin, "Roger Federer enjoys final flourish over Rafael Nadal at World Tour finals." 28 November 2010. The Guardian. Web.
150.   "Rafael Nadal 2011 Bio." ATP Tour. Web.
151.   Ibid.
152.   Hodgkinson, Mark. "Rafael Nadal's Australia Day curse strikes again as injury ends bid for 'Rafa Slam.'" 26 January 2011. The Daily Telegraph. Web.
153.   Mitchell, Kevin. "Rafael Nadal plays down hamstring injury." 26 January 2011. The Guardian. Web.
154.   "Rafael Nadal 2011 Bio." ATP Tour. Web.
155.   Newbery, Piers. "Novak Djokovic ends Nadal's run on clay in Madrid." 8 May 2011. BBC Sport. Web.
156.   Mitchell, Kevin. "Novak Djokovic rolls on with defeat of Rafael Nadal in Rome." 15 May 2011. The Guardian. Web.
157.   Newbery, Piers. "Rafael Nadal beats John Isner in five sets." 24 May 2011. BBC Sport. Web.
158.   Ibid.
159.   Mitchell, Kevin. "Rafael Nadal too hot for great rival Roger Federer." 5 June 2011. The Guardian. Web.
160.   Ibid.
161.   Ibid.

162.   Chadband, Ian. "Rafael Nadal suffers injury in fourth round defeat of Juan Martin del Potro. 27 June 2011. The Daily Telegraph. Web.

163.   "Rafael Nadal 2011 Bio." ATP Tour. Web.

164.   Clarey, Christopher. "Djokovic's Dream Made Real with Wimbledon Conquest." 3 July 2011. The New York Times. Web.

165.   Ibid.

166.   "Rafael Nadal 2011 Bio." ATP Tour. Web.

167.   Clarke, Liz. "Andy Roddick routed by Rafael Nadal and John Isner falls to Andy Murray in quarterfinals." 9 September 2011. The Washington Post.

168.   Ornstein, David. "Andy Murray loses to Rafael Nadal in semis." 11 September 2011. BBC Sport. Web.

169.   Ibid.

170.   Mitchell, Kevin. "Roger Federer struggles to accept Novak Djokovic defeat." 10 September 2011. The Guardian. Web.

171.   "Novak Djokovic claims U.S. Open crown." 13 September 2011. ESPN via The Associated Press. Web.

172.   Ibid.

173.   "Rafael Nadal seals Davis Cup win for Spain." 4 December 2011. BBC Sport. Web.

174.   Ibid.

175.   "Rafael Nadal 2012 Bio." ATP Tour.

176.   "Nadal survives Berdych scare to set book Federer showdown." 24 January 2012. The Daily Mail. Web.

177.   Mitchell, Kevin. "Rafael Nadal triumphs over Roger Federer in epic Australian Open semi." 26 January 2012. The Guardian. Web.

178.   Ibid.

179.   Ornstein, David. "Novak Djokovic beats Rafael Nadal in Australian Open final." 29 January 2012. BBC Sport. Web.

180.   Ibid.

181.   Ibid.

182.   "Novak Djokovic outlasts Rafael Nadal." 29 January 2012. ESPN via The Associated Press. Web.

183.   Briggs, Simon. "Rafael Nadal forced to withdraw from Miami semifinal against Andy Murray with with recurrence of knee tendinitis." 30 March 2012. The Daily Telegraph. Web.

184.   "Rafael Nadal 2012 Bio." ATP Tour. Web.
185.   Ibid.
186.   "Rafael Nadal beats David Ferrer to reach final." 8 June
        2012. BBC Sport. Web.
187.   Lewis, Aimee. "Nadal & Djokovic final suspended by rain."
        10 June 2012. BBC Sport. Web.
188.   Ibid.
189.   Dickson, Mike. "Seventh heaven! Nadal secures record
        French Open title with triumph over Djokovic. 11 June 2012. The
        Daily Mail. Web.
190.   "Rafael Nadal 2012 Bio." ATP Tour. Web.
191.   Mitchell, Kevin. "Rafael Nadal blasted out of Wimbledon by
        world number 100 Lukas Rosol." 28 June 2012. The Guardian.
        Web.
192.   "Injury forces Rafael Nadal to pull out of Olympic Games."
        19 July 2012. The Guardian via The Associated Press. Web.
193.   "Rafael Nadal withdraws due to stomach virus." 28
        December 2012. The Daily Telegraph. Web.
194.   "Rafael Nadal 2013 Bio." ATP Tour. Web.
195.   "Rafael Nadal beats Juan Martin del Potro in Indian Wells
        final." 17 March 2013. BBC Sport. Web.
196.   "Rafael Nadal 2013 Bio." ATP Tour. Web.
197.   Mitchell, Kevin. "Rafael Nadal crushes Roger Federer to
        show clay supremacy in Rome final." 19 May 2013. The
        Guardian. Web.
198.   "Rafael Nadal 2013 Bio." ATP Tour. Web.
199.   "Novak Djokovic 2013 Bio." ATP Tour. Web.
200.   Newman, Paul. "Rafael Nadal's epic semifinal win leaves
        Novak Djokovic distraught." 7 June 2013. The Independent. Web.
201.   Ibid.
202.   Ibid.
203.   Newbery, Piers. "Rafael Nadal beats Novak Djokovic to
        reach eighth French Open final." 7 June 2013. BBC Sport. Web.
204.   Mitchell, Kevin. Rafael Nadal downs David Ferrer for record
        eighth French Open title." 9 June 2013. The Guardian. Web.
205.   Ibid.
206.   "Rafael Nadal upset in first round." 24 June 2013. ESPN.
        Web.

207. "Rafael Nadal takes Cincinnati final." 18 August 2013. ESPN via The Associated Press. Web.
208. "Rafael Nadal 2013 Bio." ATP Tour. Web.
209. Newbery, Piers. "Rafael Nadal beats Novak Djokovic to win second U.S. Open title. 10 September 2013. BBC Sport. Web.
210. Ibid.
211. Ibid.
212. Ibid.
213. "Rafael Nadal 2013 Bio." ATP Tour. Web.
214. "Rafael Nadal 2014 Bio." ATP Tour. Web.
215. Ibid.
216. Newbery, Piers. "Rafael Nadal beats Grigor Dimitrov to make Australian Open semis." 22 January 2014. BBC Sport. Web.
217. Ibid.
218. Newman, Paul. "Floored Roger Federer complains at Rafael Nadal's grunting after losing semifinal." 24 January 2014. The Independent. Web.
219. Robson, Douglas. "Stan Wawrinka wins Australian Open over hobbled Rafael Nadal." 26 January 2014. USA Today. Web.
220. Ibid.
221. Ibid.
222. "Rafael Nadal 2014 Bio." ATP Tour. Web.
223. Ibid.
224. Briggs, Simon. "Rafael Nadal sweeps aside David Ferrer to set up semifinal against Andy Murray. 4 June 2014. The Daily Telegraph. Web.
225. Newman, Paul. "Andy Murray no match for Rafael Nadal at Roland Garros." 6 June 2014. The Independent. Web.
226. Clarke, Liz. "Rafael Nadal beats Novak Djokovic for record ninth French Open title." 8 June 2014. The Washington Post. Web.
227. Ibid.
228. Ibid.
229. "Rafael Nadal 2014 Bio." ATP Tour. Web.
230. Newbery, Piers. "Rafael Nadal beaten by Nick Kyrgios at Wimbledon." 1 July 2014. BBC Sport. Web.

231.   Newman, Paul. "Rafael Nadal's wrist injury hits preparations for Flushing Meadows." 30 July 2014. The Independent. Web.

232.   Briggs, Simon. "Rafael Nadal's withdrawal from U.S. Open heightens suspicion that his body is starting to rebel." 18 August 2014. The Daily Telegraph. Web.

233.   "Rafael Nadal: 14-time Grand Slam winner confirms his season is over." 24 October 2014. BBC Sport. Web.

234.   "Rafael Nadal 2015 Bio." ATP Tour. Web.

235.   Walton, Darren. "Tomas Berdych hammers Rafael Nadal to end 17-match losing streak." 27 January 2015. Sydney Morning Herald. Web.

236.   "Rafael Nadal 2015 Bio." ATP Tour. Web.

237.   Ibid.

238.   Briggs, Simon. "Novak Djokovic beats 'king of clay' Rafael Nadal with demolition job at Roland Garros." 3 June 2015. The Daily Telegraph. Web.

239.   Ibid.

240.   Battersby, Kate. "Qualifier Brown sends Nadal crashing out." 2 July 2015. Wimbledon.org. Web.

241.   Ibid.

242.   "Rafael Nadal 2015 Bio." ATP Tour. Web.

243.   "Rafael Nadal falls to Fabio Fognini at U.S. Open." 5 September 2015. USA Today via The Associated Press. Web.

244.   "Rafael Nadal loses to Fernando Verdasco." 19 January 2016. BBC Sport. Web.

245.   "Rafael Nadal 2016 Bio." ATP Tour. Web.

246.   McCarvel, Nick. "Rafael Nadal withdraws from French Open due to injury." 27 May 2016. USA Today. Web.

247.   Ibid.

248.   "Rafael Nadal beats Brazil's Thomaz Bellucci in Rio, will face Juan Martin del Potro in semis." 12 August 2016. Tennis.com via The Associated Press. Web.

249.   Kilgore, Adam. "Juan Martin del Potro outlasts Rafael Nadal in raucous Olympic semifinal." 13 August 2016. The Washington Post. Web.

250.   Ibid.

251.   "Rafael Nadal 2016 Bio." ATP Tour. Web.

252.   Ibid.

253.   "Rafael Nadal survives five-set thriller versus Alexander Zverev." 21 January 2017. The Guardian via Press Association. Web.

254.   Quayle, Emma. "Rafael Nadal beats Gael Monfils to make the quarterfinals." 24 January 2017. Sydney Morning Herald. Web.

255.   Ibid.

256.   Briggs, Simon. "Rafael Nadal shows off his old class to see of Milos Raonic and remain on course to see Roger Federer." 25 January 2017. The Daily Telegraph. Web.

257.   Ibid.

258.   "Rafael Nadal to face Roger Federer in final after beating Grigor Dimitrov in semi at Melbourne Park." 27 January 2017. ABC.net. Web.

259.   Steinberg, Jason. "Rafael Nadal beats Dimitrov to set up Australian Open final – as it happened." 27 January 2017. The Guardian. Web.

260.   "Rafael Nadal to face Roger Federer in final after beating Grigor Dimitrov in semi at Melbourne Park." 27 January 2017. ABC.net. Web.

261.   McClure, Sam. "Men's final preview, Rafael Nadal versus Roger Federer." 28 January 2017. Sydney Morning Herald.

262.   Ibid.

263.   Altruda, Chris. "Roger Federer Biography." 19 February 2017. Web.

264.   Ibid.

265.   Ibid.

266.   Ibid.

267.   Ibid.

268.   Ibid.

269.   Ibid.

270.   Ibid.

271.   Ibid.

272.   Ibid.

273.   Clarey, Christopher. "Roger Federer, Defying Age, Tops Rafael Nadal in Australian Open Final." 29 January 2017. The New York Times. Web.

274.   "Rafael Nadal 2017 Bio." ATP Tour. Web.

275.   Ibid.

276.   Ibid.

277.   Hodges, Vicki. "Rafael Nadal into French Open semifinals after Pablo Correna Busta retires." 7 June 2017. The Daily Telegraph. Web.

278.   Cambers, Simon. "Rafael Nadal overwhelms Dominic Thiem to reach French Open final." 9 June 2017. The Guardian. Web.

279.   Briggs, Simon. "Rafael Nadal beats Stan Wawrinka in straight sets to win 10th French Open title." 12 June 2017. The Daily Telegraph. Web.

280.   Ibid.

281.   Ibid.

282.   Jurejko, Jonathan. "Rafael Nadal loses to Gilles Muller 15-13 in fifth set." 10 July 2017. BBC Sport. Web.

Chapter 5 Bibliography

1. "Rafael Nadal vs. Roger Federer Head To Head." ATP Tour. Web.

2. Keel, Toby. "Federer: I knew from the start Nadal would become better than me." 18 March 2016. Eurosport. Web.

3. "Rafael Nadal vs. Roger Federer Head To Head." ATP Tour. Web.

4. Wallace, Ava. "U.S. Open hopes rest on possibility of first Roger Federer-Rafael Nadal match at tournament." 27 August 2017. The Washington Post. Web.

5. Ibid.

6. "Rafael Nadal vs. Novak Djokovic Head To Head." ATP Tour. Web.

7. Ibid.

8. Ibid.

9. Muthanna, Pradhan. "Novak Djokovic talks about 'special' Rafael Nadal rivalry and Roger Federer influence." 5 January 2017. International Business Times. Web.

10. "Rafael Nadal vs. Andy Murray Head To Head." ATP Tour. Web.

11. Ibid.

12. "Rafael Nadal vs. David Ferrer Head To Head." ATP Tour. Web.

Chapter 6 Bibliography

1. Nadal, Rafael. "Family crisis destroyed my heart and soul." 17 August 2011. The Daily Telegraph. Web.
2. Ibid.
3. "Rafael Nadal 2009 Bio." ATP Tour. Web.
4. Ibid.
5. "Federer Wins Madrid Open, Defeating a Run-Down Nadal." 17 May 2009. The New York Times via The Associated Press. Web.
6. Ibid.
7. Ibid.
8. Clarey, Christopher. "Nadal Is Stunned, Losing Where He Feels Most at Home." 31 May 2009. The New York Times. Web.
9. Nadal, Rafael. "Family crisis destroyed my heart and soul." 17 August 2011. The Daily Telgraph. Web.
10. Chase, Chris. "Report: Nadal's parents are back together after separation." 22 June 2011. Busted Racquet via Yahoo! Sports. Web.
11. "Rafael Nadal: the three key women – his mother, sister and girlfriend – in his life talk about the man they know." 17 August 2011. The Daily Telegraph. Web.
12. Ibid.
13. Tandon, Kamashi. "Nadal wants to have kids, values off-court relationships." 28 February 2015. Tennis.com. Web.
14. RafaNadal Foundation. Web.
15. RafaNadal Foundation. Presentation. Web.
16. RafaNadal Foundation. 2015 Annual Report. Web.

Chapter 7 – Bibliography

1. "Rafael Nadal Bio." ATP Tour. Web.
2. "Roger Federer Bio." ATP Tour. Web.
3. Ibid.
4. "Roger Federer vs. Novak Djokovic Head to Head." ATP Tour. Web.
5. Nadal, Rafael. Brainy Quotes. Web.

Printed by Amazon Italia Logistica S.r.l.
Torrazza Piemonte (TO), Italy

53877024R00078